Dear Heather,

Thanks so much for supporting our book. You have been an inspiration for positivity and resilience — both necessary for getting us through the journey of bringing our project to light.

Keep on shining!

— Hugh

THE INTRAPRENEUR'S
JOURNEY

Empowering Employees
to Drive Growth

Published by the Lean Startup Company
www.leanstartup.co

The Intrapreneur's Journey
Empowering Employees to Drive Growth

Published by the Lean Startup Company

KICKSTARTER EDITION

ISBN 978-0-578-41339-6

I dedicate this book to my loving family Michelle,
Danielle, and Dineo for their unflagging support during
our journey of creating this book. Mahal ko kayo.
Hugh Molotsi

Without the loving appreciation and support of
my family, Elizabeth, Danika, Kurt and Drew, my
contributions to this book would not have been possible.
This is for you.
Jeff Zias

Acknowledgements

Innovation is a team sport and so was the effort to turn our book concept into reality. We are grateful to the many people without whom this book could not have been completed.

For their inspiration, encouragement, and guidance during the book's journey:
Brad Smith, Eric Ries, and Heather McGough

For her invaluable contributions, diligent editing, and patient guidance to make our book stand out and become a practical guide:
Kellyn Bardeen Standley

To the innovation leaders who generously shared their lessons learned:
Mamie Rheingold, David 'Pablo' Cohn, Dominic Price, and Prachi Gupta

For their selfless contributions at critical parts of the project:
Alison Ball, Dustin Caruso, Sheila Ells, Rachel Evans, CJ Legare, Ian Maple, Danny Ortega, Isabelle Rogner, Sara Vassar, and Emily Yeager

To our especially generous Kickstarter backers:
Scott Baird, Blank Page LLC, Mlamli Booi, Philippe Boulanger, Christine Bowling, Samuel Bright, Bennie Eng, Sinan Gul, Hisham Ibrahim, Amit Jain, Jeff Langston, Ingrid Larik, Vlad Magdalin, Jason Phung Le, Erin Liman, Daniel Mak, Mariette Martinez, Jeff McGrath, Jackie Meyer, Pascal A. Miserez, Michael Robinson, Bill Sarris, Heather Satterley, Paul Shrimpling, Catherine Valentine, Barry L. Williams, and Greg Wright

To Scott Cook, Brad Smith, Bill Ihrie, Pankaj Shukla, Narinder Sandhu, Roy Rosin and the too many to mention Intuit employees who have been part of creating an amazing culture of innovation that we have had the privilege of being a part of our lives.

Table of Contents

Preface

When Steve Jobs in a 1985 Newsweek article described his Macintosh team as an "intrapreneurship", he was letting us in on a powerful insight. Companies that deliver sustainable growth by continuously delivering innovative new products do so through intrapreneurs, innovative employees who behave like startup teams in a garage, but doing their work inside an established company.

While all companies strive to be innovative, most companies inadvertently choke the efforts of their intrapreneurs through hierarchical bureaucracies that only support projects initiated from the top by senior leadership. On the other hand, companies that have a track record of serial innovation have developed a culture of intrapreneurship where intrapreneurs are nurtured and supported. These employees contribute game-changing ideas that drive growth. It is in fact the *culture*, and not just a few geniuses, that produces a track record of sustained innovation. Our book is written for people who want, or must, transform their companies by unleashing the full potential of their intrapreneurs. Because the competition is too close, the stakes are too large, and the opportunity is too great.

Now there are many books that have been written on how to develop an innovation culture, but our book is unique. We provide hands-on practical tools for implementing systemic change. Our **Intrapreneurship Empowerment Model** describes the components of an effective and sustainable internal innovation program. By following our model, your company will go from having inadequate innovation activity and a struggling innovation program, to having an innovation engine where intrapreneurs are prolifically churning out products that will drive growth. Together with a description of our model, we provide an assessment for you to use to evaluate your own company's program.

Our insights are drawn from years of experience and practical lessons learned leading innovation at Intuit, including our personal experiences with the QuickBooks Merchant Account Service and Idea Jams **[See Chapter 10: The Authors' Stories]**[1]

---

[1] Page 178

We have also had the privilege of learning from other innovation leaders at other companies including 3M, Atlassian, Google, and LinkedIn.

Our book outlines how companies can drive growth and increase employee engagement by giving employees the time, freedom, and capabilities to work on their ideas. Our work has in part been inspired by what Daniel Pink has described in his book *Drive* as the deeply human need to direct our own lives. We will show how to use design thinking and Eric Ries' Lean Startup methodology to empower employees to effectively explore their ideas. We will also show you how to overcome common pitfalls you will likely face. The typically contentious relationships between intrapreneurs and bureaucratic functional groups will be transformed into highly collaborative partnerships. We show you how to influence company leadership and co-workers by providing key resources that can serve as templates for your own communication and events.

Our book also explores unchartered territory by delving into the issues you can expect to face once your intrapreneurs are producing more good ideas than you can handle. Having more ideas than you can fund presents challenges that must be addressed. We argue that it is imperative to provide an outlet for "excess" innovation so as not to frustrate intrapreneurs and to keep the culture of intrapreneurship vibrant. It will be critical to find a home for products that have achieved traction but lack synergy or strategic fit with your company's current business unit structure. Rather than shutting down successful innovations, we discuss housing them in an emerging products division (like IBM's Emerging Business Opportunity Division) or utilizing external corporate venturing to spin out startups with an option to reacquire them in the future (like Cisco's "Spin-along" approach).

How to Use This Book

There are three ways for you to consume the materials we have provided for you:

1. The Prizmic Parable - For an easy-to-read narrative that describes our lessons learned, we have written a fictional parable about Patty Porter, an innovation leader at the software company Prizmic as she works to empower employees to innovate. The parable is loosely based on our own experiences and stories we've heard from other

innovation leaders. All characters are fictitious and any resemblance to actual persons are coincidental and not intended. We also provide commentary throughout the parable to explicitly call out important lessons and when appropriate, call out references that have informed our perspectives. You can also flip to the key resources (described below) as they come up in the parable to give you a deeper understanding.

2. The Intrapreneurship Empowerment Model - We provide a description of the six components required to build an effective and sustainable internal innovation program. We also include an assessment tool that you can use to evaluate the state of your own innovation program with diagnoses and recommended remedies.

3. Key Resources - When you're ready to launch your innovation program (or strengthen it), we provide materials you can use as a starting point. We are "open sourcing" these resources and encourage you to modify them to suit your own company's context.

Navigating the Book

Here's a map of what to look forward to in each chapter:

1. **The Intrapreneurship Empowerment Model** - This chapter provides an overview of our model and how it was developed. Our assessment tool with sample diagnoses will help you determine your company's opportunities for improving your innovation culture and which following chapters in the book to focus on.

2. **Time and Freedom** - Learn how a company that has started to become too bureaucratic can jump start its innovation culture by giving employees the time and freedom to work on their own ideas. We include the business case for intrapreneurial time programs and how to rebut the common arguments you will hear against them.

3. **Dedicated Innovation Team -** A dedicated team of stellar innovation coaches and "change drivers", sitting at the center, is required for intrapreneurial time programs to maintain their momentum. A dedicated innovation team drives programs that build and scale the company's intrapreneurship muscles.

4. **Design Thinking** - Innovation is not just about creating new products for customers. Internally facing intrapreneurs can deliver process and infrastructure improvements with significant bottom

line impact. By teaching all your employee Design Thinking, every employee across the organization will have the tools to innovate effectively.

5. **Open Collaboration** - Many companies are secretive and jealously guard their nascent activities from leaking out. This secretive culture makes it difficult for employees in different groups to collaborate. Instead, we will show how an open exchange of ideas with collaboration between employees, customers, and partners greatly catalyzes innovation.

6. **Lean Experimentation** - When employees start contributing ideas, the next question is how to sift through all those ideas. A common approach is to anoint a panel of senior leaders to judge ideas. We will show why judging ideas is a futile exercise and may actually squash your best ideas. Instead, employees should run experiments that yield data that will make the value of their ideas self-evident.

7. **Align for Yes** - In a culture where employees are given autonomy to innovate, senior leaders must still play a critical role in breaking down the organizational barriers that get in the way of intrapreneurs. Leaders must ensure that every part of the company, including non-product creating functions, are aligned as enthusiastic partners in innovation. Instead of "no" being the default answer to difficult questions, the prevailing practice should be an exercise on how to get to "yes."

8. **Culmination: Intrapreneurship Week** - We show you how all the elements of the Intrapreneurship Empowerment Model are brought together through an operating mechanism we call Intrapreneurship Week where intrapreneurship teams develop minimum viable products for in-market testing in one week.

9. **Epilogue: Sustaining Success** - Once your innovation culture is up and running, you are likely to experience the paradox of success - your innovation engine is generating many more good ideas than your company can invest it. It is imperative for the health and sustainability of the culture that companies strategically manage their "excess" innovation. We will describe two approaches for solving the paradox.

10. **The Authors' Stories** - learn our own personal intrapreneurship stories and how they have informed our passion for empowering all employees to innovate.

CHAPTER 1
INTRAPRENEURSHIP EMPOWERMENT MODEL

The Innovation Paradox

Every single large company was once a small startup. This small startup fueled by a powerful idea and driven by resourceful entrepreneurs created an innovative new product that gave the budding company a foothold into the market. With success came revenue and employee growth. The startup that was once scrappy and nimble now had to adapt to success by introducing organizations and processes to efficiently manage the larger, more complex business. With their large number of customers and fiduciary responsibilities to shareholders, bureaucracy became a necessity to make sure rules were followed. The bureaucracy ultimately squashed the company's ability to innovate (we will explore later in more depth how bureaucracy is an impediment to innovation).

This is the "Innovation Paradox" – the notion that innovation drives growth and that growth squashes innovation. Clay Christensen has described how very few large companies have over time been able to consistently deliver breakthrough "disruptive" innovations.

The Paradox

The Model

Imagine a workplace where every employee feels they can do the best work of their lives. They are encouraged to autonomously develop insights as they work with customers and products. Those insights lead to ideas which they share with their fellow employees, with corporate partners, and even customers, refining and improving them along the way. Each employee can choose which idea they are passionate about and join teams to quickly develop Minimum Viable Products for in-market experimentation. After several iterations, certain teams have customer validated data proving their products have merit and will help drive company growth. With self-evident data in hand, each team pitches their products to senior leaders who enthusiastically bless them for formal funding.

Such a workplace is not some imaginary utopia. We've observed many aspects of this vision in several innovative companies that empower frontline employees. With the Intrapreneurship Empowerment Model, we are providing you a framework to bring these best practices to your company. The Intrapreneurship Empowerment Model is the antidote to the Innovation Paradox.

The Intrapreneurship Empowerment Model consists of the following six facets:

1. **Time & Freedom** – Employees are given self-directed time, carved out from their day jobs, to work on their own projects. Without available time, all the freedom in the world and access to resources won't make a difference. Companies often give employees this time by scheduling innovation time in the form of Hack Days, or by baking a percentage of free time into the work backlog. Employees are given autonomy to explore ideas they are passionate about. When employees gain a sense of freedom, they are more creative, feel more engaged in the work they are doing, and are able to take a bolder approach when trying solutions.

2. **Dedicated Innovation Team** – All employees are supported by a central, internal team of supportive coaches who provide the tools, mindset and guidance needed to accelerate the company's innovative progress. These 'capability builders' are often located at the center of the company under someone with a job title like "VP of Innovation".

3. **Design Thinking** – Employees use Design Thinking principles to be effective innovators. These principles include: A relentless focus on customers where intrapreneurs seek to have deep customer empathy; an exhaustive consideration of possible solutions before selecting one; and refining that solution through rapid iterations of

prototypes and deployments with customers.

4. **Open Collaboration** – Employees can easily find out what other employees are working on in their self-directed projects, provide feedback, and form teams across organizational and geographic boundaries. A healthy system of collaboration makes the innovation culture transparent, best practices and key learnings can propagate broadly, and overall progress quickens.

5. **Lean Experimentation** - Employees are provided the tools and infrastructure to test their ideas. Decisions are driven by data instead of the leader's opinion. Employees are able to move quickly from idea to hypothesis to experimental results. The speed of this cycle largely determines the overall innovation capability of the organization.

6. **Align for Yes** – Employees are given resources, tools, training, and senior leadership mentoring to develop their self-directed projects. A formal process is in place allowing projects to "graduate" to officially funded initiatives. If leadership support fails to assist teams that need and deserve the help, promising innovations will "die on the vine." But when the kind of leadership support that correctly aligns, unblocks, and resources small innovative teams, a multitude of innovations can move forward to dramatically improve business results for the company.

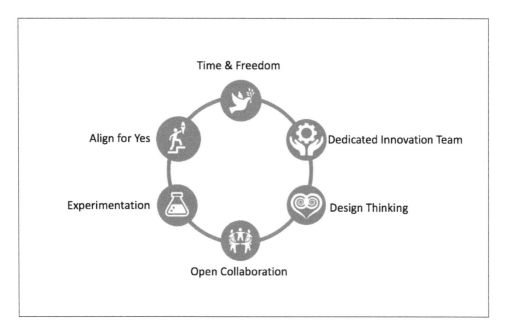

Cultural Impact

Giving employees **Time and Freedom** engages employees to connect their passion and purpose to work projects. When employees are shown the goal, have internalized the mission, but also have the freedom to broadly consider the ways to best make their own, unique contribution, results improve. In fact, the employees that have both the time to think and the freedom to go beyond the status quo establish a culture of creative productivity that resoundingly beats the competition.

A **Dedicated Innovation Team** sets the common language, tools, standards, and infrastructure for employees to be "serial intraprenuers". With the dedicated team, the evergreen innovation programs driven - or at least assisted - from the center of the company serve as a solid foundation for a culture of continuous innovation.

Design Thinking is the powerful set of principles that help employees achieve innovation mastery. A culture of customer obsession is the holy grail of companies that might truly change the world for customers while obliterating competitors,and Design Thinking enables intrapreneurs to go deeper and deeper into actionable customer empathy, resulting in breakthrough solutions that can delight customers.

Open Collaboration facilitates the cross pollination of ideas, sharing of insights and solution components across an organization. When employees learn to cross boundaries and work in ad hoc agile teams, silos disappear and the organization finds a new "gear." With a healthy system of open collaboration, customers, partners, and employees can all connect to produce broader and more powerful innovations than any that might occur in isolation.

Experimentation improves both the effectiveness of employees and senior leaders. Employee become engaged in the decision-driving process by creating and collecting the data that drives good decisions. Leaders shift to setting bold visions and freeing employees to experiment with customers to discover what truly works. The corporate culture based on experimentation eschews antiquated power structures and instead places evidence and customer empathy at the center of all decisions.

Finally, **Align for Yes** forms the foundation for a culture that enables intraprenuers to make fast progress. In a culture where employees are given autonomy to innovate, senior leaders must play the critical role of breaking down the organizational barriers that get in the way of entrepreneurs. Leaders do this by ensuring that every part of the company, including non-product creating functions, are aligned as enthusiastic partners in innovation. Instead of "no" being the default answer to difficult questions, the prevailing practice becomes a cross-functional, boundary-eliminating exercise on how to get to "yes."

The Intrapreneurship Empowerment Model Assessment

Many internal innovation programs we've observed fail to properly develop each of these facets. Although we believe having any kind of innovation program is better than doing nothing, we hope this assessment will help show more organizations an effective path forward.

Please answer each of the following questions:

1. At my company we have full autonomy to work on our own ideas.

1	2	3	4	5
Strongly disagree	Somewhat disagree	Neutral	Somewhat agree	Strongly agree

2. I feel like I can work on my own idea without asking permission.

1	2	3	4	5
Strongly disagree	Somewhat disagree	Neutral	Somewhat agree	Strongly agree

3. Management affords me self-directed time to work on my own ideas.

1	2	3	4	5
Strongly disagree	Somewhat disagree	Neutral	Somewhat agree	Strongly agree

4. I feel like innovation is systematic and well-understood here.

1	2	3	4	5
Strongly disagree	Somewhat disagree	Neutral	Somewhat agree	Strongly agree

5. We have a strong set of programs and resources to enable innovation.

1	2	3	4	5
Strongly disagree	Somewhat disagree	Neutral	Somewhat agree	Strongly agree

6.   I can get the innovation help I need (learning from customers, coaching and advice, etc) .

1	2	3	4	5
Strongly disagree	Somewhat disagree	Neutral	Somewhat agree	Strongly agree

7.   Our teams truly focus on primary research leading to customer empathy.

1	2	3	4	5
Strongly disagree	Somewhat disagree	Neutral	Somewhat agree	Strongly agree

8.   Rapid prototyping is built into our culture.

1	2	3	4	5
Strongly disagree	Somewhat disagree	Neutral	Somewhat agree	Strongly agree

9.   Employees at our company know what design thinking is and apply to as habit.

1	2	3	4	5
Strongly disagree	Somewhat disagree	Neutral	Somewhat agree	Strongly agree

10. Employees at our company can easily find out what other employees are working on in their self-directed projects.

1	2	3	4	5
Strongly disagree	Somewhat disagree	Neutral	Somewhat agree	Strongly agree

11.   Employees often form teams across organizational and geographic boundaries.

1	2	3	4	5
Strongly disagree	Somewhat disagree	Neutral	Somewhat agree	Strongly agree

12.   Our company encourages open collaboration on ideas with customers and partners.

1	2	3	4	5
Strongly disagree	Somewhat disagree	Neutral	Somewhat agree	Strongly agree

13.   We continuously run experiments on our products.

1	2	3	4	5
Strongly disagree	Somewhat disagree	Neutral	Somewhat agree	Strongly agree

14.   Our product decisions are driven by data from experiments.

1	2	3	4	5
Strongly disagree	Somewhat disagree	Neutral	Somewhat agree	Strongly agree

15.   Generally, sign-off on running an experiment is made at the lowest level possible, usually by team members.

1	2	3	4	5
Strongly disagree	Somewhat disagree	Neutral	Somewhat agree	Strongly agree

16.   Our employees are given resources, tools and training to develop their self-directed projects.

1	2	3	4	5
Strongly disagree	Somewhat disagree	Neutral	Somewhat agree	Strongly agree

17.   At our company, we regularly receive senior leadership mentoring for our self-directed projects.

1	2	3	4	5
Strongly disagree	Somewhat disagree	Neutral	Somewhat agree	Strongly agree

18.   Our self-directed projects often "graduate" to officially funded initiatives.

1	2	3	4	5
Strongly disagree	Somewhat disagree	Neutral	Somewhat agree	Strongly agree

Scoring

Time & Freedom	Total for questions 1, 2, and 3	
Dedicated Innovation Team	Total for questions 4, 5, and 6	
Design Thinking	Total for questions 7, 8, and 9	
Open Collaboration	Total for questions 10, 11, and 12	
Experimentation	Total for questions 13, 14, and 15	
Leadership Support	Total for questions 16, 17, and 18	

For each facet:

- If you score > 12 points, that is an area of strength for your organization
- If you score between 10 and 12 points, this is an area where your organization has made good traction but has an opportunity to improve
- If you score < 10 points, this is an area of improvement for your organization.

The goal over time for your innovation program is to be strong in all six facets.

Diagnoses

Here's our diagnosis of what can result from incomplete innovation programs:

Where's the money?

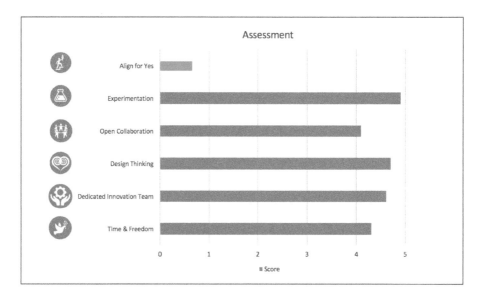

Often a company can find a way to offer time and freedom, and perhaps even a pinch of collaboration and experimentation here and there, but fail to support their employee innovators. Frequently this lack of support looks like an inability to resource and fund new innovative initiatives.

Here's the typical situation: Business unit leaders, at any given time—except perhaps a "planning season" annual fire drill—are locked into meeting pre-ordained quarterly and annual objectives. Leaders who meet these goals are successes. And you know what we call the ones who fail to meet their goals. So the centuries of corporate cues revolving around *"it's all about execution, we need to hit our plan, discipline is key, fortitude and brutal prioritization are the way,'* solidly anchor the status quo. This means that new emerging ideas stand nary a chance. Perhaps if the idea stemmed from the brain of the GM herself, then something may happen. But what business leader in their right mind would routinely violate committed plans to breath life into some tiny, yet promising, pipe dream?

Companies, like people, often need to find a rocky bottom. Pain isn't generally good. But the necessary pain associated with developing "new ways of working" is of high value.

The inability to move projects past early prototypes is similar to slamming one's head against a wall. Nobody thrives in that environment. For growth—and sanity—something must change. Promising new initiatives must be supported.

When companies put a structure in place to enable leadership support for new, innovative work, new healthy habits can form. The entire corporate culture may transform, the catalyst of transformation being the emotion of hope. Hope for new and emergent offerings. And hope for the kind of support that nourishes innovative employee's souls.

Enslaved by the regular job

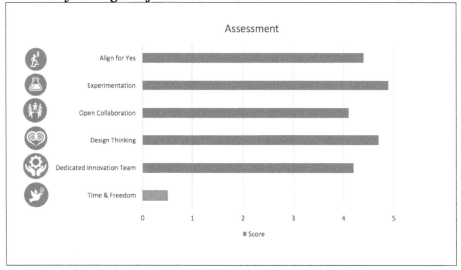

The research of Harvard Professor Teresa Amabile, the writings of Daniel Pink, and industry research concerning workforce engagement, clearly illustrate that giving employees time and freedom can effectively heighten employee engagement.

Yet so many companies stay laser focused on the mindset of short-term wins, thereby failing to protect any time at all for employees to exercise intellectual freedom. Employees need to create, to make progress, to call upon personal strengths, to own a significant spot in the sun, and to make a personal dent in the universe (no matter how small). These feats are unachievable within the force field of runaway micro-management. Companies that do offer "some" time may hold events that employees can sign up for to develop their projects with some funding to run in-market experimentation. These "Hackathons" can be high-energy and drive engagement. However, no time is set aside to continue work on the project after the event. The effectiveness of the events over time start to diminish as the novelty factor wears off. Innovation becomes episodic instead of "always active."

Companies must break free of the "hyper-control disease" by launching the Whitespace time and Hack days programs. Once the top-down expectation is set—that employees are creative, innovative, invent the future of the company—employee time and freedom gains a toehold.

Leaders still hold power and exercise control. But, with leaders as strategic catalysts, coaches, and meritocratic green-lighters, employees retain a strong, invigorating sense of freedom.

Without innovation time and freedom for employees, the stack of post-it notes sitting on your desk might not exist. Gmail wouldn't be open in your browser tab, and Google would be devoid a few tens of billions of Adsense revenue. Graphene—and its associated Nobel prize—wouldn't exist.

We're all busy. Nearly always. But setting aside the time for employees to think creatively, to be better, to autonomously improve the lives of coworkers and customers, is not just one of the greatest gifts a company can offer. It is a gift that returns exponential dividends.

I feel so alone

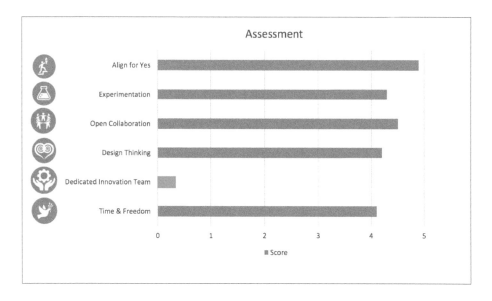

Employees need the resources to build, and maintains, a thriving culture of innovation. This type of thriving culture doesn't just accidentally happen. In fact, without specific focus and dedication to building and running this internal "operating system" enabling intrapreneurs, any adventurous employee trying to boldly innovate for customers may feel like they're a lone pioneer left to fight their way across rugged and uncharted terrain.

But dedicated innovation team tasked with building supporting innovation capability across the company solves this problem. The dedicated team defines and runs programs that inspire, guide, protect and curate the work of intrapreneurs.

Excuse me, but what am I supposed to do?

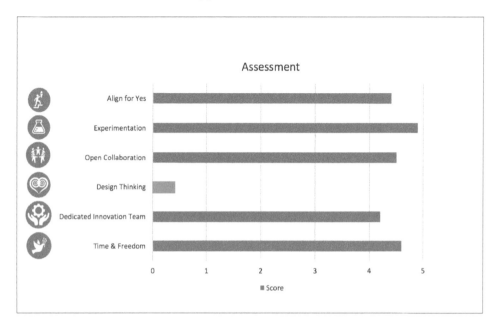

Companies that don't communicate and teach the core principles of Design Thinking leave employee floating, rudderless, in the challenging seas of customer needs. Employees need to know how to think from a customer perspective, how to formulate specific and narrow understanding of customer needs, how to broadly ideate and then quickly test a multitude of ideas, all the while staying focused on solving to dramatically improve customers' lives. Otherwise, time is wasted as employees develop or redevelop mindsets and mechanism that may or may not work.

The most successful companies think customer back -- are literally obsessed with serving the customer well -- while rapidly exerimetaint their way to great decisions that drive customer delight and corporate growth. Without grounding the "how we work"in Design Thinking, your company can become anything but "design-led", which leads to inside out thinking and poor business results.

Difficult to find a team

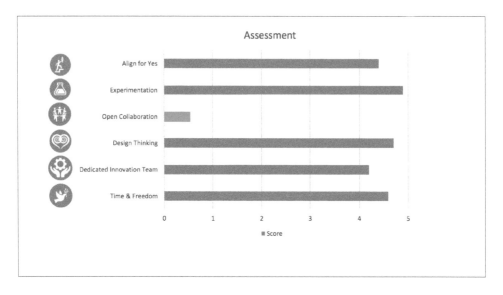

These companies provide time and support for self-directed project but don't have a formal system in place that lists projects, connects like-minded intrapreneurs, and better enables small innovation teams addressing a key challenge.

In this type of non-collaborative environment, employees are limited to recruiting team members from the community of people they already know. Or they may go it as lone wolves, which only works out if you have all the hacker, designer, visionary, and hustler skills packed into the brains and fingertips of one or two people. That is rarely the case.

Additionally, without the transparency afforded by a culture and toolset of broad collaboration and active communication, multiple teams might be trying to solve the same problem.

Prizmic suffered from this "difficult to find a team" syndrome until Boris and Patty vowed to find a state of the art tool for Prizmic-wide collaboration. After settling on the "BrightIdea" innovation management tool, the whitespace task force found that teams knew how to find team members, share customer insights, and align to the top Prizmic customer-need-driven innovation challenges published by senior leaders.

Running on Opinions

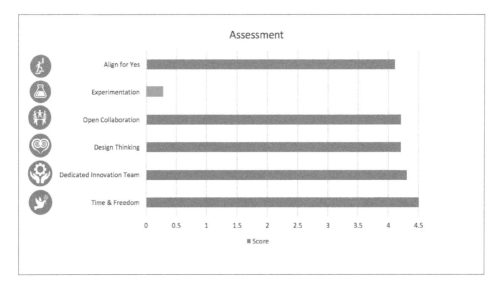

In these companies, decisions are mostly "gut calls" often relying on the opinions of senior leaders. Without a sincere dedication to decisions by experiment, human nature prevails. And, sadly enough, human nature is to postulate opinions and sheer conjecture until the "argument" is won. The most senior leader usually wins. And all people tend to base opinions on board, unsubstantiated assumptions.

The only cure? The inherent meritocracy of experimentation not only creates a playing field seeded with customer actuals (real behavior), but engages all employees in the decision process. Sure, the final calls may be made by leaders in the role as decisions approvers, but employees and leaders, at all levels, work to develop the customer behavioral evidence that drives the best decisions.

To emphasize the importance of decision by experiment, consider the fact that the most innovative of ideas often, at first, seem ridiculous. As Albert Einstein said, "If at first the idea is not absurd, then there is no hope for it." And Einstein knew a thing or two about breakthrough thinking.
When frontline employees have these ideas that challenge conventional wisdom, they face an insurmountable challenge for getting funding and support. These companies are destined to miss out on the most disruptive

ideas their employees have in spite of their aspirations to be innovative.

The one advantage of a corporate engine that "runs on opinions" is that the opinion-well never goes dry. Opinions are the most renewable resource known to mankind. Conversely, solid evidence of customer behavior is real work to obtain. Your barrels of customer evidence will in fact dry up here and there … and refilling isn't trivial.

But here's the bald-faced truth: opinions will drive you quickly—with reserve fuel tanks filled to the brim—to the wrong destination.

Better to use the finicky fuel. It's more difficult to harvest, but it takes you to the right place. Making that turn to fast growth depends upon your fuel source.

We rock!

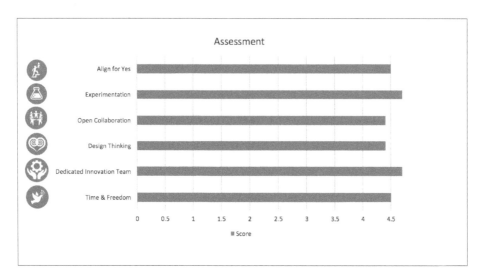

"We rock!" companies are delivering on all facets of the innovation model, with a regular pipeline of employee ideas that become new products delivering growth.

Prizmic, like your company, needed to complete a *Hero's Journey* to reach this "we rock" zone. Increased employee engagement was rooted in the move to offer Whitespace time, driving increased **freedom**. Hack Days and Jams carved out available **time** for employees to move sparks to ideas to experiments to offerings that improve customer's lives. Intrapreneurship Weeks identified the need—and eventually the solutions—for rapid **experimentation.** Legal checklists allowed employees to experiment without the constant threat of bureaucratic reprimand. Prizmic Labs and the dedicated attention to employee **open collaboration** lubricated the company's innovation and experimentation engines. Finally, with all business and functional groups in the company viewing their roles as driving innovation, Prizmic established the **align for yes** mindset needed to properly support and coach these new offerings.

What Prizmic put in place wasn't perfect—and it wasn't easy. But their systematic approach is enough to leave their opinion-based, bureaucratic competition in the dust.

We believe Prizmic's journey is the right journey for every company seeking continuous, speedy growth.

Try it. Measure it.
And grow.

CHAPTER 2
TIME AND FREEDOM

"It's not about 'having' time.
It's about making time."
- Unknown

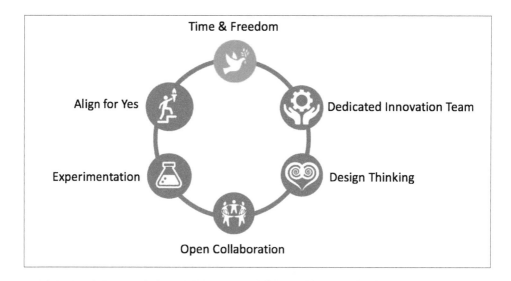

Introduction

The most valuable currency for intrapreneurs is the time and freedom to work on their own ideas. But managers in your organization will bring up a number of reasons to resist providing time and freedom to employees. They will feel that schedules are too tight, that priorities are already set so "why wander off priority", and that employees will do nothing more than squander their time and freedom on blue-sky, unfocused, time-wasters. However, the absolutely most innovative companies in the world, for example Google, Apple, 3M, Atlassian, Intuit, and a host of others, have enabled time and freedom for their intraprenuerial employees. They do this with Hack days and 20% time style programs -- which we refer to as "Allocated-time" programs, characterized by an allocated percentage or slice of employee's time -- to be used to work on their own innovative ideas. These programs can be as simple to start as a one day Hackathon, or as complex as a combination of Hack Days, allocated percentages of "time to be intraprenuerial", and inspirational innovation contests.

Feeling Restless

It was the spring of 2005 and Patty Porter, who had just completed her tenth year at Prizmic Software, was feeling restless. She'd had a good run at Prizmic where she started as an entry-level engineer and now was a highly recognized Principal Engineer reporting to the VP of Engineering. She had seen the company, which made productivity software, grow from 150 employees to over a thousand. In that time, the company had gone public and the stock had split once, giving her a financial windfall which gave her the luxury of not having to worry about a next paycheck for a few years.

With summer approaching, Patty was considering moving on from Prizmic and spending the summer abroad with her husband Rick and their two young sons. Even though she loved her job — she admitted it was the biggest passion in her life outside of her kids — she found herself enjoying work less and less as the company had grown bigger.

The work itself was still challenging and engaging. Prizmic, with headquarters in Menlo Park California, was a desktop software company but realized the future was cloud applications. Patty was asked to lead an initiative to design the architecture and select the technology which would allow the company's new cloud applications to work seamlessly with their desktop applications. Prizmic couldn't afford to leave their two million customers behind as they transitioned to the cloud.

However, bureaucracy meant that work progress was painfully slow while Patty spent most of her day in meetings with different levels of management. The cloud technology decision was critical to the company's success and everyone seemed to have an opinion and wanted to have a say in the decision.

Even harder for Patty to bear was watching how difficult work was for the junior engineers. Their work assignments were rigidly managed and they were not being given any latitude to be creative. All new product features were specified and assigned by product management. Designs were reviewed by the architect and before software engineers could check in their code, a group consisting of an architect, two peers, and a quality engineer had to review it and sign off. Even the simplest of code changes could take three days. Patty lamented to her boss, VP of Engineering for the Consumer Division

Rowan Sandhu, how different things were from when she was a junior engineer. "It used to be, if I had an idea, I could walk over to the PM's cube, talk it over, and have it implemented and checked-in that same day!"

Rowan would patiently listen and respond: "Yes Patty, but we're a much bigger company now and that cowboy culture just doesn't scale."

"But this bureaucratic culture doesn't scale either! Look how long it takes to get anything done! And if an engineer has a great idea, they might as well forget about it because there's no way they'll get anything approved given our huge backlog of features.

"Take for example Ilya. He came to me last week to show me a table flyover widget he'd developed after seeing feedback from customers that the table was too difficult to read. It was a perfect solution! But Sally [QA manager] said there were no resources available to test the widget and Janice [Product Manager] refused to make it a priority for the release. So the result is we're not going to ship his working code that our customers desperately need! And Ilya is now being scolded for not focusing on his assigned work!"

Rowan highly valued Patty and worried that she was a flight risk. That would be a huge loss for the company. She was a great role model for team through her passion and hard work and her knowledge of the product would be irreplaceable. He knew she was making good points but hadn't yet figured out how to channel her frustration productively.

Commentary: The Insight Decision Divide

Most companies strive for growth. And as if that goal weren't challenging enough, the growth needs to be continuous and sustainable. But so many companies are failing to tap into one of their most powerful assets: the ideas in their employees' heads. These companies strive to innovate, and they look to their leaders for game changing ideas. But executives are likely to be spending most of their days in meetings with other executives.

Front-line employees are more likely to be working with customers and the products customers use each day. This realization is lost on so many companies. And the resultant truth stings a bit: Frontline employees are more likely than senior executives to come up with game-changing innovations.

The everyday experiences of frontline employees provide them with key insights. These employees see the customer struggles. The employees often observe customer behavior, hear the word of mouth, and absorb hints pointing to key opportunities. But the decision makers remain abstracted from the front-line, the place where reality tends to congregate. This "insight-decision divide" typical in most companies means many employees' great ideas remain hidden.

The evidence of these "hidden assets" becomes most apparent, and most painful, when employees leave a company to launch their own startup to turn their ideas into products. But the hidden assets also exist in less obvious forms. For example, an employee may have an idea for a killer new product feature which the company fails to act upon until a competitor implements it. Another common example is where employees foretell the fatal issues that a project will face long before that project is canceled.

Here are just a few examples of companies missing huge opportunities by failing to take advantage of their hidden assets. In many of these instances, these startup founders have stated that they would have been quite happy to have built the product for their former company. But, you guessed, the former employer had no interest in the idea:

Hewlett-Packard and the Apple I: <u>Steve Wozniak begged HP five times</u>[1] to make the Apple I. They turned him down five times. Fortunately, Steve Jobs saw the potential of the personal computer and together the two Steves created Apple Computers. And here's a fun data point: In March 2016, Apple's market cap hovers just below $600B while the combined valuation of Hewlett Packard Enterprise and Hewlett Packard Inc is around $50B.

Real Networks and the iPod: Tony Fadell took his idea of a hard-drive based digital music player to Apple after clashing with the CEO of Real Networks.[1] The iPod would eventually lead to Apple's resurgence.

PayPal and Youtube: Founders Chad Hurley, Steve Chen, and Jawed Karim left PayPal to start Youtube when they realized how difficult it was to share videos online. Google acquired Youtube for $1.65B2 in stock in 2006.

For many companies, tapping into frontline employees' ideas has fueled their sustained growth. By empowering frontline employees to work on their own ideas, these companies have been able to develop new products and key new capabilities.

Here are a few examples of frontline employee innovations:

The Facebook "Like" Button: Developed by engineers Boz, Justin Rosenstein, Leah Pearlman, Ezra Callahan, and Akhil Wable at a Hackathon. The "Like" button overcame resistance that it would reduce activity feed engagement. The employees experimented and were able to prove that the like button actually increased the number of comments. The Sony Playstation: Engineer Ken Kutaragi overcame his management's perception that gaming was not for serious companies. After spending many hours tinkering with his daughter's Nintendo Famicon console, he developed a Playstation prototype that eventually

---

[1]http://bizjournals.com/atlanta/blog/atlantech/2013/01/woz-i-begged-h-p-to-make-the-apple-1.html

won senior leader support. The Sony Playstation went to market and soon became one of the world's most valuable brands.

ELIXIR guitar strings: W.L. Gore employee Dave Myers hypothesized that coating guitar strings with the company's miraculous ePTFE polymer would make the guitar strings more durable and comfortable to play. It turned out that the coated strings weren't only more comfortable but had an unexpected benefit: they held their tone longer than any other guitar strings. Guitarists voted with their wallets. Dave's guitar strings, branded ELIXIR strings, were, and still are, the world's #1 best selling acoustic guitar string.

Atlassian's Jira Service Desk: At a "ShipIt" Hackathon in 2013 employees Andreas, Nick, Mike, Ross, and Scott came up with the idea to use Jira (agile development tracking software) for tracking customer service issues. Jira Service Desk soon became the fastest growing product in Atlassian's corporate history.

Giving employees autonomy to innovate is a timeless best practice. For example, we can look back to when Thomas Edison was inventing the incandescent light bulb. Edison's Menlo Park Research Park lab started out in typical 19th century factory fashion: Edison did the thinking and assigning of tasks. Then his subordinates did the work. But when the lab hit around 60 employees, everything changed. Edison, already working more than 80 hour weeks, realized he must reconfigure the lab into a series of small teams. Each team had a scientist leader; Edison quickly began to see the value of the teams themselves driving concepts, experiments, then reporting summarized results back to him.

Edison pushed on employee autonomy, and the light bulb and electrical delivery system were born. Clearly impressed with his employees, Edison, decided to give a 5% business equity stake to lead lighting scientist Francis Upton.

We see that it is often a natural consequence of corporate growth to have this large "insight-decision divide" between leaders and the employees who are close to customers. But when companies leave this divide and bureaucratic culture in-place, bad things happen. Employees tend to ideate, become frustrated, and peel off to invent the future, leave their (often beloved) former employer behind.

But, some of the most successful and transformative companies in history (Sony, Facebook, Atlassian, W.L. Gore, Edison Electric) have harnessed the power of front-line employees to drive amazing levels of growth. The insight-decision divide is a natural consequence of traditional corporate hierarchy, but cannot be allowed to impede progress. This divide must be bridged. The good news is that bridging the divide is not impossible. All that's needed is the right know-how and a few bold decisions. Then the bridge can be constructed with sensible mindsets and clear tactics.

Prizmic is in a difficult position. Patty, a key employee, is loose in the saddle and likely to leave. Rowan is concerned but unsure what to do. The Prizmic culture has truly become bureaucratic and molasses-slow. For example, Ilya's flyover widget became entangled in red-tape, all progress was blocked, and he was scolded for not focusing on his "work". Employees are frustrated.

What will Prizmic do?

Employee Engagement

Meanwhile, one of the key items of interest for the senior leadership team was *employee engagement*. Every year, Prizmic would conduct an employee survey which included a set of questions that measured how engaged employees were with their work. These questions included "Are you proud to work at Prizmic?" and "I'm determined to give my best work at Prizmic every day."

CEO Noel Spence had noticed that Prizmic's engagement score had fallen for three years in a row. "This is not sustainable. We have tough challenges ahead of us and we will not succeed if our people are not engaged. I want to hear ideas of how we can turn this around," he asked at his staff meeting.

Noel understood very well the power of employee engagement. Engaged employees are more productive so improving engagement improves the bottom line.

CTO Sebastian Veksler was also familiar with the importance of engagement. At his previous company, he had listened to a presentation from consultants who shared research showing that companies which have employee autonomy programs tend to have higher engagement.

Sebastian spoke up: "Noel, what if we give every employee time to work on their own ideas? Many people have the misconception that more money is the best way to motivate employees. Dan Pink in his book *Drive* cited experiments which proved that for creative, intellectual work, financial incentives can actual have an adverse effect on performance. Instead, he made the case that one of the best ways to incentivize performance is to give employees autonomy."

The CIO, Randy Mercer said, "Did I hear you correctly? With all our projects that are running behind, did you just suggest giving time to employees to play around?"

"It's not for playing around. It's for working on their ideas. Most employees have good ideas on how to better solve customer problems or improve internal processes but they don't have time to do anything with them because they're busy with their day jobs," Sebastian explained. "And studies have shown that companies that implement freedom programs have higher employee engagement."

"I think I'm with Randy on this one," Noel said, "How do we know this won't be a big waste of company resources?"

"We won't be the first company to take the plunge," Milton said. "Google has a 20% program where every employee can spend a day a week on their own projects. That's where GMail came from – it was an employee's idea. They borrowed that idea from 3M where every employee gets 15% of their time."

VP of HR Harriet Ingram joined the discussion. "I've heard good things about the Google program. It's created a buzz in the industry which also helps them with recruiting. Millennials in particular are attracted to companies where they have freedom to be creative. None of our competitors has a program like that. It would be great to be first."

"But our employees are not the same as Google's employees. I don't even know if they'll know what to do if we leave them to their own devices," objected Randy.

"*Au contraire*, I think our best employees would be thrilled to see that Prizmic cares about their ideas and is willing to invest time so they can explore," said Sebastian.

Dan Lewinsky, GM of the Consumer Division said: "You know, you'll be surprised how much frontline employees know on how to improve the business but we don't listen enough. You've heard the story of how at Amazon, Jeff Bezos discovered they were shipping tables that were getting damaged during shipment?"

"No, I haven't heard that one," Noel responded. "Please share."

"Well Bezos was at a call center handling customer support calls…" Dan started to say.

"Wait, why one earth was the CEO of Amazon doing customer support?" Randy asked.

"Oh, at Amazon, all senior leaders including the CEO are required to take two days of customer service training every other year," Dan said. Randy had a look of disbelief on his face. "Don't worry Randy, they always have an experienced customer service agent listening in and available to jump in if they need help.

"On one particular call, as soon as the customer's order appeared on the screen, the experienced agent leaned over to Bezos and whispered 'She's going to want to return that table,' pointing to one of the previous orders. Sure enough, the customer told Bezos 'I want to return the table.' It turned out the top of the table was scratched because it had been packaged poorly. After handling the return and finishing up with the customer, Bezos turned to the agent and asked 'How did you know that the customer was going to return the table?'

'Oh that table always gets returned,' replied the agent.

"It turns out that the agents knew things that the executives had no clue about. Bezos then instituted what they call the 'Andon Cord' where any customer service agent who notices repeated instances of customers complaining about problems with a product can pull that product from the website."

Janice Hult, the VP of Customer Support said. "Yes, that's a legendary story in the customer support world. That's why I've been harping on all of you to spend some time in the call center and take calls."

"Well let's stay on topic. I certainly don't want to concede that our employees are not as creative as Google's. Can we try a small scale experiment to see if giving our employees self-directed time would work for us?" Noel asked.

"We could try it for a limited amount of time in one of our groups," said Harriet.

"I like that idea. Sebastian, since this is your proposal, let's start with a product development group. Let's try it for a couple of quarters and see what happens. Will you take the lead in making that happen?" Noel asked Milton.

"Yes, I'll be happy to do it!"

"Alright. Any other ideas on how to increase engagement?"

The Freedom Guinea Pig

Every month, Sebastian led a meeting that included all the heads of engineering at Prizmic. He shared the CEO's concerns about falling engagement and how an autonomy program could help. "Now I know many of you will be skeptical about giving employees time to do whatever they want, but I don't want to ignore the research. I don't know if a program like that will work at Prizmic but I'd like to try. What if we start with just one division? Who would like to be the guinea pig?"

Without hesitation, Rowan raised his hand. "The Consumer Division will do it!" An autonomy program sounded like exactly what his group needed and he knew just the person to lead the effort to roll it out.

Commentary: The Business Case for Intrapreneurship

Giving employees time and freedom to work on their own ideas makes great business sense. Imagine this case: One of your employees has an idea that may dramatically impact the fortunes of your company. What is the ONE thing she will need more than anything else? Time. She needs the time where she's free to work on her idea. And believe it or not, she values this time and freedom more than she values incremental amounts of money.

"Intrapreneurial Time" is what we call the time and freedom employees get to work on their own ideas and push beyond the status quo. Intrapreneurial Time comes in various forms. One common, and often easy to execute type of Intrapreneurial Time Program is a Hack Day. Hack Days are immersive, full day experiences where your intrapreneurs develop ideas, prototypes or experiments that will help the company. Generally Hack Days last one day, although sometimes these Hack Days or Hackathons stretch across a multitude of days.

A second form of Intrapreneurial Time comes to life when companies support Allocated-time. Examples of effective Allocated-time programs are 3M's "15% time rule", Google's "20% time", Intuit's "Unstructured Time" and W.L. Gore's "10% Dabble time". With Allocated-time programs, employees develop the "mindset" of seizing the permission to add value in unexpected ways. Without an Allocated-time program, employees are much less likely to try enough things and won't experiment broadly enough to create new breakthrough innovations.

When you allow employees to have Intrapreneurial Time, three primary business benefits come to life:

- **Increased Employee Retention** - Engagement and retention increase significantly in companies that give employees the time and freedom to be intrapreneurial.

- **Increased Innovation** - companies that give their employees more freedom are 20 times more innovative than companies with low freedom scores (according to the LRN research and other studies we we will explore). The more innovative breakthrough products drive revenue growth and increased profitability.

- **Increased Growth and Profitability** - companies that allow their employees more freedom are 10 times more likely to financially outperform companies with low freedom scores. Innovation alone is a fine thing, but high-freedom employees are also specifically more effective at driving financial wins because they are intrinsically motivated.

Increasing Employee Retention

Intrapreneurial Time gives employees a boost in intrinsic motivation, which in turn leads to increased job satisfaction. And when employees have high job satisfaction, retention is also high!

A 2006 study run out of Cornell University[1] recorded the activities of 320 small businesses. Half of these small businesses consistently demonstrated old fashioned command and control management practices, but the other half gave employees time and freedom. The researchers referred to the difference in the two groups as stark differences in "autonomy". The businesses that exercised command and control, giving the employee little or no time and freedom, experienced three times the turnover of the businesses that gave employees time and freedom.

The autonomy from Intrapreneurial Time heightens employee's intrinsic motivation. And when intrinsically motivated, these employees are happier and more satisfied with their jobs than other employees. It's clear, highly engaged, intrinsically motivated[2] employees stay. And this is important because all companies need to retain their top talent. Without solid retention numbers, especially of their most creative and high potential employees, companies lose focus, progress slows, and business

---

[1]http://digitalcommons.ilr.cornell.edu/cgi/viewcontent.cgi?article=1108&context=articles
[2]http://mcser.org/journal/index.php/mjss/article/download/3957/3873

targets are missed.

As a case in point, Quicken Loans offers employees an Intrapreneurial Time program called "Bullet time", a four hour weekly time allocation where employees can work on any idea they want to. Quicken Loans boasts an amazingly low 13% annual turnover rate.

Increasing Innovation

Intrapreneurial Time increases employees' intrinsic motivation which leads them to do more creative work, resulting in more innovative outcomes. And the reasons that Intrapreneurial Time increases innovation are surprising. In the 1990's, Harvard Professor Teresa Amabile led a team of researchers to conduct a unique experiment with artists. The researchers asked 23 painters and sculptors to submit some of their past works to an evaluation committee of experts (museum curators, art historians, gallery owners, etc.). Each artist randomly submitted 10 of their commissioned works and 10 non-commissioned works. Amabile presented the 460 pieces of art to the experts.

Amabile and her colleagues reported that - "Our results were quite startling. The commissioned works were rated as significantly less creative than the non-commissioned works, yet they were not rated as different in technical quality."

Bestselling author Daniel Pink[1] leveraged Amabile's[2] research to assert a powerful conclusion[3] within his book *Drive*: "if you want breakthrough work in your organization, carve out a small island – a week or even just a few days – for non-commissioned work."

So we see that Intrapreneurial Time heightens employee's intrinsic motivation. And when intrinsically motivated, employees do more creative work.

We repeatedly see that Intrapreneurial Time acts as an innovative creativity accelerant. Facebook's "Like" button, Edison's light bulb, the Nobel prize winning "Graphene" material, 3M's Post-it notes, and so many other impressive innovations came from employees having the

---

[1]http://youtu.be/u6XAPnuFjJc   [2]https://bit.ly/2S7Aolc   [3]https://bit.ly/1GkmEq1

time and freedom to be intrapreneurs.

The most innovative companies empower employees to bring their passionate, creative selves to work each day. And these are the employees that tap into their passions to work on their own ideas, thereby innovating the creative future of their companies.

Increasing Revenue and Profits

Companies giving employees Intrapreneurial Time can enjoy faster and more profitable growth. A 2013 study from the Legal Research Network (better known as LRN, a compliance, legal and ethics research organization) showed that companies that allowed their employees more freedom were 10-20 times more likely to outperform companies with low freedom scores. LRN studied over 1,000 employees at hundreds of organizations and contrasted the 21% of the organizations who scored in the "high employee freedom" range with those in moderate and low freedom categories.

Yes, the data also implies that 79% of companies have an untapped potential to significantly increase revenue and profits. If yours is one of those companies, we're here to help. Without a doubt, you want to be like the top 21% of companies in the "high freedom" category that are reaping revenue and impact from their intrapreneurs' projects.

Intrapreneurial Time programs empower employees to drive innovative growth. Google, as a special case in point, reports that 50% of all Google products have come from 20% time. 25% of Google's revenue comes from these 20% time projects. This data, although impressive, is underselling the reality. Google is essentially a company that leverages superior search technology to drive large revenue streams. That was the first and "best" business Google has. So when you look at what "new things" drive most revenue, 20% time shines much brighter. Without Intrapreneurial Time (in the "Allocated-time" 20% time form) Google would be lacking the inventive and strategic growth breakthroughs coming from GMail, AdSense, News, and Android mobile.

As another specific example, Intuit provides Intrapreneurial Time as Unstructured Time as well as Hack Days, Hack Weeks and Innovation Challenge contests. Intuit's Intrapreneurial Time has generated over 500 "graduates", meaning innovation projects that started in Intrapreneurial TIme but progress to be fully supported and shipped to internal or external customers.

Success stories abound. Australian software maker Atlassian's thriving business recently added JIRA Service Desk as it's fastest growing product line. JIRA Service Desk was born during one of Atlassian's quarterly "Ship it Days" where teams self form and hack on new experimental ideas.

Atlassian has long been a fast growing company with a culture that fosters innovation. In a personal interview with Head of Atlassian R&D Programs, Dominic Price, he pointed out that 'ShipIt' is more than just a hackathon. "Many employees here at Atlassian describe ShipIt as '24 hours of opportunity'. Atlassians at every level participate, from last week's hires to senior executives and the CEO. And we're all given the same challenge: drop our day-to-day to identify and solve problems."

At a ShipIt day in 2013 employees Andreas, Nick, Mike, Ross, and Scott had a new, adventurous idea. "What if we used JIRA to meet an important new need, a need that's outside of JIRA's current area of focus?"

They centered on an idea and spent 24 hours hacking together a simple portal to create 'issues' in JIRA. The implications were large. This "JIRA Service Desk" could use tickets to track any issue. What if this ticket tracking could transform the world of customer service? Most companies had issues with customer service, right?

They were in fact right. JIRA Service Desk was born. Customers soon flocked to JIRA Service Desk. A big unmet need was met, and the product became the fastest-growing product in the Atlassian's history.

The impact of JIRA Service Desk now goes beyond the product itself.

Atlassian recently re-organized around a three point model of product types. The three product pillars are: (1) JIRA Software (designed for software developers), (2) JIRA Core (for users who want to use the product outside of software developer needs), and (3) JIRA Service Desk (the wildly popular customer service product).

This new product line, which started at ShipIt days and was then built and grown during Atlassian 20% time, is now one of the three strategic cornerstones of the company.

The business case for giving employees Intrapreneurial Time is clear. When employees have time and freedom, retention is higher, the company becomes more innovative, and revenue and profits increase. But, in most cases this "change" means overcoming tough opposition within your company. Change is hard. People, to a large degree, want to maintain the status quo, keep their current place in the sun, staying with their current lower-risk and reasonable-reward way of living. Inertia must be overcome. You need to understand the pushback and have powerful arguments at the ready. Anticipating all the inertia and arguments against time and freedom will help you break through this "great wall of corporate inertia".

You've Been Recruited!

A week later, when Rowan called Patty to his office, she thought he wanted to talk to her about the broken build (another constant problem brought on by having a large software engineering team).

"We've figured out what broke the build and it will be fixed before lunchtime," Patty said, before a chance for any pleasantries.

"I didn't call you to talk about the build. Sebastian has asked the Consumer Division to implement an autonomy program and I want you to make it happen."

The next hour Rowan described all he knew about autonomy programs and employee engagement. Patty listened intently and became more excited as she imagined the possibilities. An autonomy program will be the perfect antidote to Prizmic's crippling bureaucratic culture. An engineer like Ilya Smirnov could work on his ideas without worrying about being scolded. Patty was sold.

Rowan had already talked to Allison Tan, the VP of Product Management, sold her on the idea and asked her to identify a PM counterpart to work with Patty. "I want you to work with Derwin Reese and both of you should assemble a team to work on a proposal. I want us to move quickly. Please send me a draft before the end of the week."

When Patty got home that night, she told her husband Rick about her conversation with Rowan.

"So what are you thinking?" Rick asked.

"I want to take it on but if I do, it means no summer abroad."

"You know what? The summer abroad thing was your thing. I was just going along. If you're happy at work, that's cool too! Plus, I think the kids were kind of bummed they were going to miss out on their summer camps. Actually, I'm kind of relieved I don't have to ask for time off from my work!"

Patty and Rick had a great relationship and she was thankful that he was flexible.

Patty was pleased to find when she talked to Derwin, he was equally excited about the opportunity. They brainstormed a list of engineers and product managers to include in the team. Patty made sure they included at least one person they thought would be skeptical about the approach. She had learned in her career you want to hear the naysayer's points *before* you roll out the proposal.

Two days later, they held their first meeting. There were eight attendees including Patty and Derwin. After explaining the idea, they were both taken aback by the lack of excitement in the room. Ilya, who was on the top of Patty's list to invite, was the first to speak.

"Giving us time to work on our ideas is cool but when will we be able to do anything? We have so many meetings during the day, it's barely possible to get our assigned work done."

The rest of the attendees jumped in. Yes, meetings were a huge burden. Not having to attend so many meetings would be a huge boost to their engagement! Pankaj Aron, a senior engineer, made a suggestion. "If I could just have one afternoon free of meetings, that would be huge. What about if we mandate no meetings on Friday afternoons?" The group loved the idea. The proposal would not just outline the autonomy program but also include a no-meetings stipulation.

"What should we call this program?" Derwin asked.

The group bandied around a bunch of names but none of them seemed to capture the essence of the autonomy program. "What about whitespace?" Patty said. Whitespace had been used in the company to refer to adjacent opportunities to the business that the company wasn't actively working on. The logic is that many employees would use their autonomous time to work on whitespace ideas.

"In graphic design, 'white space' is what allows the information on a poster or label to come through more easily.. It is the visual 'rest' which allows the information to demand fewer cognitive resources."

"In fact, it is the reason lowercase letters are easier to read. Putting text entirely in uppercase provides less variation in the variation in the negative space around the letters."

The name wasn't perfect but it worked for everyone. Then came the work of defining how Whitespace Time would work. The proposal included specifications like:

1. Employees would spend up to 20% of their time each week self-directed (this would eventually be negotiated down to 10% by Rowan and Allison's staffs).
2. Employee could spend time doing the following:
    a. Creating new solutions for customers
    b. Improving internal processes and tools
    c. Learning new skills
3. Employees would let their managers know what they were working on in their Whitespace Time. This was not for approval — but to keep the managers in the loop in case they could help.

The following week, Rowan sent out a message to the entire Consumer Division announcing the launch of Whitespace Time **[See Key Resource: "The Whitespace Time Announcement"]**[1]. That was the easy part. Next, was how to get employees to use the time productively.

Hack Days

Patty and Derwin and the attendees of the first meeting decided to meet weekly as a Whitespace Time Task Force to plan activities. First on the agenda was a series of Q&A sessions where employees could learn more about Whitespace Time and get answers to their questions. Boris Vinogradsky, a QA manager with a thick Russian accent offered to bring Russian chocolates to the sessions to encourage people to attend.

Patty got a mischievous look on her face. Boris was often fun to tease. "I didn't know Russians ate chocolate."

"Ha! I can also bring vodka if you want!" said Boris.

Over the course of the next two weeks, the task force hosted four Q&A sessions. The bribe of chocolate was probably unnecessary given all the sessions were standing room only. The following were some of the most common questions they heard:

Can I really work on anything I want? (Yes, but use good judgment — choose ideas that will help the business)
- I'd like to learn more about advanced HTML/CSS development. Who will pay for the development tools? (Your manager will, just ask).
- I'd like to form a book reading club. Is that allowed? (Yes, that fits under learning new skills).

Boris, who was proving to be the life of the party in a largely introverted group, had a suggestion when the task force met. "Whitespace time is cool but we should have a Hackathon! My wife is an engineer at Yahoo! and she said they were a lot of fun. Teams spend 24 hours building working code and then a panel of judges pick the best ones and the winning teams get prizes."

Derwin immediately liked the idea. "That sounds cool! What kind of prizes?"

"I think they gave out iPods," Boris replied.

"But I already have an iPod. What would I do with another one?" Ilya said.

"What, you don't have somebody in your life you could gift that to?" Patty said.

"Yes, but I'd be more motivated to get something I could use."

Pankaj said, "Who cares about the prizes. We could give out gift certificates for all I care. I think just the recognition would be a big deal for me. I'm more interested in who will be doing the judging."

"At Yahoo!, I think it was the VPs," said Boris.

"We see Rowan and Allison all the time. Imagine if we could get Sebastian!" said Patty.

"Or how about Noel? Having the CEO at the Hackathon would be really cool!" said Derwin.

"Ooh! Do you think he'd come?" asked Boris.

"We'll never know if we don't ask" said Patty.

Patty ran the idea by Rowan of having a Hackathon and getting Noel and his staff to judge the event. Rowan was very supportive. "Try and get on Noel's calendar as soon as you can. He has a busy schedule so if you want him to attend, he'll need some lead time."

Patty was pleasantly surprised to find how easy it was to get 30 minutes on the CEO's calendar. When she met with Noel to run the idea by him, not only was he supportive but he had his own ideas.

"You know our move from desktop to the cloud is crucial to our survival. We have to move fast or risk being displaced by an upstart who isn't saddled with legacy technology. But when I ask my leaders how we can speed up our migration, I don't hear any new ideas. How can we get our most creative employees to come up with new solutions?" Noel asked.

"That sounds like a challenge! Maybe you should set the stage and context for the day in your opening remarks" said Patty.

"A challenge? I like that word. You think employees will be motivated by me talking about it?"

"Absolutely! We like hearing directly from you compared to what gets filtered down the organization."

Six weeks later, the first Prizmic Hack Day was held on a Thursday and turned into a big event.

[See Resource: Hack Day Sign Up Form][1]. Even though attendance

---

[1] page 196

was not mandatory, most of the 250 employees in Allison and Rowan's organizations signed up to participate. Participants self-organized into teams of two to six. There were about a dozen employees who needed help from the task force finding a team. An online spreadsheet was set up for each team to sign up and register the idea they were working on.

They started at 8 am with breakfast. The task force reserved four conference rooms so teams could spread out and have room to work. The biggest room served as the Hack Day headquarters for speakers and presentations. Boris played the role of MC during the course of the day. Noel spoke at 9:00 am to issue his challenge to the teams — "Help accelerate our journey to the cloud." Teams were asked to decide on their ideas before lunch and then develop their idea pitches or prototypes before the pitch outs at 4pm.

During the pitch outs, each team had two minutes to present their ideas to the panel of judges which included Sebastian, Rowan, Allison and Dan Lewinsky, the GM of the Consumer Business. Pankaj was the strict timekeeper but with almost thirty teams, the presentations took almost an hour-and-a-half.

The judges huddled for about ten minutes and announced a grand prize winning team ($1,000 gift certificate for each team member) and two runner up teams ($250 gift certificate for each team member).

Every participant received a certificate for participating in the Hack Day. The winning team consisted of a senior architect Vikram Agrawal and four junior engineers. Their idea was a working prototype of the desktop productivity app synchronizing contacts with the web server in real-time using PPP (Point-to-Point Protocol). The approach was much simpler than the synchronization engine being developed to keep the web and desktop databases in synch. Vikram had been advocating this approach for several months before the Hack Day to no avail. He was visibly pleased to get public vindication for the idea.

The Hack Day was broadly considered a big success. GM Dan Lewinsky and his staff decided to institute Hack Days every quarter and encourage employees from every function to attend. Later that year, after the latest annual employee survey results were released, employee engagement was up for the first time in four years with several employees mentioning Hack Days among their most positive experiences at work.

Company-Wide

After a few months, the GM of the Enterprise Division, Lindsey Badal had heard so many positive things about Whitespace Time, she decided to launch it in her division. One of the Whitespace Time projects, "Voice-It," enabled users to take voice-annotated notes. Voice-It was a hit with executives and became a formally funded initiative. When it was eventually released to customers, it was a feature that none of Prizmic's competitors had. The VP of Sales, Rafael Hernandez, estimated that feature alone helped drive 30% of the sales growth that year.

At the 2006 Prizmic Annual Company Meeting, CEO Noel Spence awarded Patty, Derwin, and Boris the Prizmic Spirit Award for their contributions to the company culture by introducing Whitespace Time to the company. After presenting the award, what Noel said next took most of the company by surprise.

"Whitespace Time has been a big success for the Consumer and Enterprise Divisions. Employee Engagement is up and employees are coming up with innovative solutions to our biggest challenges. We always knew Prizmic had some of the brightest and most innovative minds anywhere. So many of you have phenomenal ideas. We just need to get out of your way! There is no question that Whitespace Time works. So I'm declaring from this day on, Whitespace Time is available to use by every employee in every part of the company. From this day forward, may imagination guide you to greatness!"

What a difference a year makes. Patty couldn't imagine that last year she had been considering leaving Prizmic. Now she felt like her career was at an all-time high. The company recognition for Whitespace Time was nice but what was even more meaningful was playing a role in improving life at work for Prizmic employees. Even though she had enjoyed a career of accomplishments at Prizmic, she considered Whitespace Time her crowning achievement.

Commentary: Countering the Arguments Against Making Time for Intrapreneurship

Any proposal involving transformational change will encounter resistance. You should expect a proposal to give employees time and freedom to work on their own ideas to face significant pushback. Intrapreneurial Time will be seen by some as undermining leadership's decisions on what problems to work, or as fiduciarily irresponsible, or as simply ineffective. Effectively influencing your organization will require being prepared to address these concerns.

The following are a list of common pushbacks to Intrapreneurial Time with effective rebuttals:

Intrapreneurial Time Undermines Leadership's Decisions

Here are a number of ways you might hear the pushback that leadership's decisions are being undermined:

- Carving out time for employees to work on their own ideas will put our already tight projects at further risk.
  Employees will work on unimportant things instead of things key to the business

- We developed our priorities for a reason!

Earlier in this chapter, we discussed how scheduling one's own work is a critical factor leading to a deepened sense of intrinsic motivation. This notion will run counter to most managers' experience which involves tightly managing employee schedules and will therefore be unlikely to change many minds. However, you can make a convincing argument by talking about employee engagement and productivity.

Employee engagement is the extent to which employees feel passionate about their jobs, are committed to the organization, and put discretionary effort into their work. It turns out that most American workers are not engaged in their work. This issue should be seen as a crisis. Lack of engagement means lackluster productivity, weak creativity, and — when you consider how much time people spend at work — the absence of a happy and rewarding life.

And disengaged employees produce sub-par work. A Gallup study from 2013 followed the differences in performance between engaged and actively disengaged work units, and the differences in performance were vast. Work units scoring in the top half on employee engagement nearly doubled their odds of success compared with those in the bottom half.

Further, according to a Harvard Business Review published study from 2012, low engagement leads to decreased overall business results. The companies associated with low levels of employee engagement showed 33% poorer annual operating income and 11% lower annual earnings growth.

So given the high correlation between productivity and engagement, how does a company increase engagement? LRN's study of 1,000 employees across a multitude of companies, led by Professor Caterina Bulgarella, showed companies that grant employees a high degree of freedom outperform low freedom peers by between 10X and 20X.

Your rebuttal can thus be summarized by the following: *By carving out time for employees to work on their ideas, we will increase their engagement. Increasing employee engagement will result in a dramatic improvement in productivity in their assigned work which will more than compensate for the time they spend on their own ideas.*

Intrapreneurial Time is Fiduciarily Irresponsible

Here are a number of ways you might hear the pushback on the costs of an Intrapreneurial Time program:

- We can't afford a program like that. Multiply 20% of how much we pay employees in a year and you get an astronomical expense!

- We've already declared we should be "putting more wood behind fewer arrows" (funding fewer projects means they can be resourced more generously). Intrapreneurial Time will give birth to more projects we can't afford to fund.

The logical flaw in the expense argument is that intellectual work is a zero-sum game:

"In game theory and economic theory, a zero-sum game is a mathematical representation of a situation in which a participant's gain (or loss) of utility is exactly balanced by the losses (or gains) of the utility of the other participant(s). If the total gains of the participants are added up, and the total losses are subtracted, they will sum to zero."

The time we spend on innovation is not zero-sum because the value created in that time is not uniform across all employees and activities. In fact, the relatively small amount of effort that leads to the discovery of a new product line for a company is infinitely more valuable than the considerable effort a large team spends on an ultimately failed initiative.

In Chapter 1 we discussed how many companies fail to capitalize on their hidden assets - the great ideas that are in their employees heads. The opportunity cost represented by hidden assets dwarfs the costs of an intrapreneurial time program. One successful intrapreneurial project like Atlassian's Jira Service Desk will pay for several years worth of intrapreneurial time.

When a company has decided to stop "peanut butter spreading" resources amongst too many projects, the imperative to select the right projects becomes even more critical. New insights from Intrapreneurial Time will help ensure the company is making good resource allocation decisions.

Your rebuttal summary: *Innovation is not a zero-sum game. The value we derive from our Intrapreneurial Time program will more than pay for the costs.*

Intrapreneurial Time is Ineffective

Here are a number of ways you might hear the pushback that
Intrapreneurial Time programs are ineffective:

- But Google's 20% time program was cancelled and must be a
  failure

- People are too busy with their assigned work to find time to
  work on their own ideas.

- So many companies run hackathons, but they don't produce
  anything of value

- Most employees won't know what to do with the time and will
  just goof off.

Google's 20% Time has been maligned by many as "120% Time". How
will busy employees who are already working more than 40 hours a week
find time to work on their own ideas? Furthermore, Google's perceived
cancelation of 20% Time is seen as an indication that the program is
ineffective.

In fact, Google's 20% Time is still in place although according to Laszlo
Bock, their former HR leader, only 10% of employees use it[1]. The
perception that the program has been canceled came after the Google
Labs team was disbanded in 2011. At the time, Google leaders thought
that Labs type innovation work should align within divisions
- for example GMail Labs - so the central team was no longer needed
to nurture 20% time and support experimentation processes. But what
they failed to consider was that without the Google Labs team, support
for internal innovators would dwindle. And the damaging perception
of, "I guess 20% time isn't going to really happen any more" would
heighten. Without the Google Labs team, true entropy of the culture of
experimentation, freedom, and time for intrapreneurship could kick in.

---

[1]http://businessinsider.com/google-20-percent-time-policy-2015-4

In spite of these challenges, Google continues to be a shining example of the effectiveness of Intrapreneurial Time. As indicated earlier, 50% of Google's products and 25% of revenue come from projects birthed in 20% Time. These wins include even more recent products like Google Now and the Android Watch.

Of course there are bad ways to run Hack Days but as the Atlassian JIRA Service Desk example proves, the upsides are tremendous.

Your rebuttal summary: *Intrapreneurial Time programs at companies like Atlassian, Intuit, and Google have proven to be very effective and to this day, continue to deliver positive results.*

Horizon Planning

A number of days after Noel Spence had announced Whitespace Time was for everyone, Freda Roberts, a Director of Finance, reached out to Patty for a meeting. When they met, Freda explained that the Finance group was trying to figure out how to reconcile Whitespace Time with Horizon Planning.

Patty was familiar with Horizon Planning, a framework that had been introduced to Prizmic two years prior. Horizon Planning is a portfolio management framework to help a company balance short and long term investments with the goal of sustaining profitable growth.

At Prizmic, Horizon 1 (H1) products referred to their "adult" large established businesses like the Prizmic Enterprise Productivity Suite, which in the last fiscal year brought in $450 million in revenue with a product organization of 80 people. The primary goals for H1 product teams were revenue and profit growth.

H2 products referred to their "teenager" fast growing emerging businesses like Prizmic Field Agent, a cloud-based solution which in the last fiscal year brought in $12 million in revenue which was more than double the previous year's $5 million in revenue. The Field Agent team had a product team of 30 people, and is typical for H2 products, was not yet profitable as they invested in customer acquisition. The primary goal for the H2 product teams were revenue and customer a and eventual profitability. H2 products graduated to H1 once they demonstrated they had validated they had a sustainable growth model and profitable business.

Horizon 3 (H3) initiatives were their "infant" new product initiatives that could still be in the ideation stage or could be testing an early product with a limited set of customers. Prizmic Vendor Manager is an example of an H3 product. It has no revenue and had just launched a pilot release to 12 customers with the goal of gradually expanded the release over time. The goal of H3 product teams is to achieve superior "Love Metrics" which include demonstrating the product is delivering the intended customer benefit, that customers are actively using it (not just trying it once or twice and abandoning it) and positive word-of-mouth (the customers using the product would recommend it to friends and family).

"So I assume you're familiar with Horizon Planning?" Freda asked.

"Yes, my manager presented this to our team a couple of years ago," Patty replied.

"Great! Our question is how should we think about Whitespace Time projects? Are they H3s? I hope I'm not coming across as anal retentive, but ten percent of all employees' time is a significant investment and we'd like to know how to track it."

"Oh I don't think that's anal at all! It's a good question and I hadn't really thought about it. I don't think it makes sense to call Whitespace Time projects H3s because you would be grouping together formally funded initiatives with these self-directed time projects which are very different to me," Patty responded.

"Well, we've found the Horizon Planning framework to be really useful and it would be great if we could fit Whitespace in there somewhere."

"What about calling them H4s?" Patty asked.

"Say more."

"Well, if you think about the framework, some H3s gain traction, grow and become H2s. Similarly, some H2s will grow and become H1s. We can think of Whitespace Time projects as a pipeline of options for H3s."

"That sounds really interesting." Freda reflected for a moment. "But doesn't that imply that management will only look at Whitespace Time projects when considering new H3s? That doesn't seem to be process today? It seems like H3s come from a mandate from high up the ranks."

"I see your logic," Patty responded. "However, I don't think H3s have to exclusively come from Whitespace Time…"

"But if none of them do, the model is not valid!" Freda interjected.

"You're right. We'll have to start socializing the idea that senior leaders should consider employee ideas when deciding on what new H3s to launch."

"OK, I'm happy to work with you on adding 'H4s' to our Horizon Planning framework," Freda responded and then smiled. "I'll leave it to you to convince management to consider Whitespace Time projects as options for H3s. Good luck with that!" **[See Resource: Prizmic Horizon Planning Model]**[1].

"Oh thank you very much!" Patty replied with a laugh.

Patty wasn't too worried. With the success of Voice-It, she felt that other worthy Whitespace Time projects would naturally get prime consideration for formal funding. With the success of Whitespace Time, she felt rejuvenated and was already starting to think about what her next Prizmic challenge

---

[1]Page 260

should be.

Conclusion

You need your employees to be highly engaged intrapreneurs. And the most valuable currency for intrapreneurs is having the time and freedom to work on their own ideas.

We've seen that giving employees time to work on their own ideas will lead to significant payoffs. But, when rolling out an Intrapreneurship Time program, you're sure to encounter pushback from some stakeholders. Change is hard, and some employees and leaders will be concerned that a time and freedom program will distract people from current priorities, defocus the current efforts, and slow overall progress. But these concerns are theoretical in nature, and looking at the performance of companies that have Intrapreneurship Time programs indicates otherwise. So you need to respond with the stories and data points that illustrate the true value of time and freedom.

You can take a stepwise approach to make time for intrapreneurship in your company. The best and most achievable first steps are to give intrapreneurs time through Hack Days and Allocated- Time. We recommend starting with Hack Days, then using the momentum to progress to Allocated-Time.

When you take the steps we recommend and influence your company to move forward, you will create the time and freedom for your employees to be intrapreneurs. And companies staffed with highly-engaged, intrapreneurial employees are hard to beat.

CHAPTER 3
DEDICATED INNOVATION TEAM

"Only three things happen naturally in organizations: friction, confusion, and underperformance. Everything else requires leadership."
- Peter Drucker

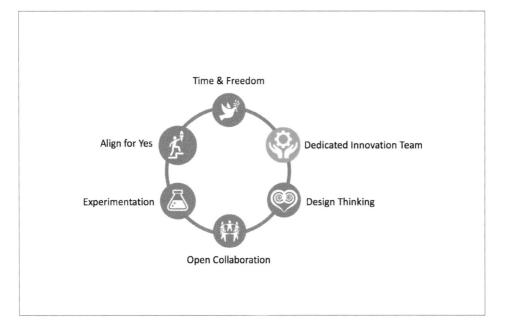

Introduction

If you watch detective shows on TV you learn that the best sleuths, at least every few episodes, mutter something like "follow the money." The corporate world isn't completely different. How your company allocates resources is the best way to see what is happening, what is "priority".

So why then do most companies say "innovative is top priority" while failing to resource it? The answer is usually one of blinders, not bad intent. Companies assume that teams will innovate just fine on their own. Spending money on things like central support for customer learning at first seems unnecessary. Likewise for the programs that teach design thinking skills, prototyping, and in-market experimentation. But these capabilities must exist in any company wishing to enable intrapreneurs.

Companies must invest in this capability-building infrastructure. Otherwise innovation is just a platitude, an unfocused thought, a lip-serviced fad. Your intrapreneurs are standing by to build your future. Show leadership, truly prioritize your intrapreneurs. Make supporting intrapreneurship somebody's day job. Or a group of "somebody's" day jobs. Give intrapreneurs the dedicated innovation support they deserve.

The Downturn

When the housing bubble burst in 2008, there were repercussions across the entire economy and Prizmic was not spared. Over half of Prizmic's business came from Fortune 1000 enterprises, almost all of which started curtailing spending in the late fall as the severity of the upcoming recession started to hit home.

For CEO Noel Spence and his staff came the difficult reality that surviving the downturn would require the first layoffs in the company's history. It was bad enough to let go of loyal employees but worse to release them into the worst job market in a generation. Come October 2008, 15% of the workforce were eliminated. Noel took some solace in giving the impacted employees generous severance packages (some companies were simply issuing pink slips).

On the bright side, Noel believed that if Prizmic could survive the downturn, the company would come back in an even stronger position. By the time the economy recovered, he anticipated many of their weaker competitors would be out of business. More importantly, their cloud strategy would be fully deployed, setting the stage for the next decade of growth.

With that in mind, Noel decided it was time to curtail resources on their desktop products and cease new feature development. Whole groups were eliminated and replaced by much smaller teams responsible for fixing bugs and addressing customer issues. With the desktop products in maintenance mode, related marketing activities were also curtailed. In the words of Jim Collins ("Good to Great"), Prizmic had "sold the mills" and was now banking their entire future on the cloud business.

Patty and all the members of Whitespace Time task force were all considered valuable employees indispensable to the company's future. They were each assigned to critical initiatives to increase the pace of new feature development on the cloud products. In Patty's case, she was asked to work with the Mobile Division, which had been a startup acquired earlier in the year.

The layoffs did bring painful losses. Patty's now former boss Rowan Sandhu was one of the executives impacted. Even though Rowan was well liked and had enjoyed a successful tenure at Prizmic, his skills were viewed as much better suited to developing desktop software with annual releases. With cloud software, Prizmic was releasing server updates every month. GM Dan Lewinsky believed Rowan was in part the reason why executing the cloud strategy was taking longer than planned. Patty was devastated at the news. She considered Rowan the best boss she'd ever had.

Patty and Rowan met for coffee during his last week. He was surprisingly upbeat. "Don't worry about me. Prizmic gave me a great package and it's going to give me plenty of time to figure out what's next."

Rowan did have advice for Patty. "I don't think you've realized your full potential. You should take more risks and play outside of your comfort zone. This work you're doing in the Mobile Division is important and interesting, but I think you're ready to take on a bigger leadership role."

The Acquisition

Makeni Inc was a startup of 80 employees who had developed a popular mobile productivity app. Milton James was their brash twenty-something year old CEO who proudly boasted of their over 100,000 and growing number of active customers. He predicted mobile apps would supplant desktop and web software and eventually they would disrupt Prizmic's business. Prizmic had been slow to react to the release of the iPhone and developing a smartphone strategy for their cloud applications. Although they had a couple of mobile projects, it was clear they weren't moving fast enough and startups like Makeni would be a threat. Even though many members of Noel's staff had misgivings about Milton, Noel felt it was imperative to push for an acquisition to make up for lost time. Even though Makeni had lots of customers, most of them used the free version of the product and profitability was a way off distant dream. Being acquired by a company like Prizmic was the most logical exit for Makeni.

After what was at times contentious negotiations, Makeni was acquired by Prizmic for $49 million. The process did not endear Milton to the executives involved in the negotiations. They would bristle when he would say "Prizmic is a stodgy old-school company that doesn't get mobile. You need us to save your future."

Noel's personality was a huge contrast to Milton's. Noel had a very modest nature and would patiently listen to other opinions. Milton was quick to voice an opinion and brag about his accomplishments. Noel figured perhaps Prizmic needed a jolt of new energy and even though Milton could be hard to take at times, he might light a fire under Prizmic that would speed up the evolution of the company. Noel made Milton the GM of Mobile Division and was responsible for developing all of Prizmic's mobile products.

Patty would report to Alan Overfield, the former CTO of Makeni who was now the VP of Engineering for the Mobile Division. Because of Patty's long history at Prizmic, the idea is that her involvement would speed up the integration of the mobile applications.

Like most Prizmic people, Patty wasn't a huge fan of Milton's. This despite the attempt to break the ice by having lunch. Patty didn't like how hard it was to get a word in edgewise. Furthermore, when she tried to explain what Whitespace Time was to Milton, he was very dubious. "Why the heck would we give employees time to fool around? We have tons of work to do and can't afford the distraction."

Patty started to explain the connection between giving employees autonomy and employee engagement and how engaged employees were more productive. It was an explanation she had given dozens of times before but this was the first time it did not convince.

"My employees are already engaged. Come to our offices at 8pm. Almost everyone is still here working. We're not a stodgy old company where you need to artificially inflate engagement!"

Patty wondered how many of Milton's employees were truly engaged or were just waiting around for their options to vest. She didn't feel there would be any point to asking the question. Milton didn't seem interested in learning about anything the Whitespace Time Task Force had accomplished.

At least her new boss Alan seemed to be a wonderful guy. He was down to earth and wore shorts to work every day. He seemed genuinely interested in what Patty had to say and frequently would tell her how much she was needed to make the mobile integration work. Patty was amazed that Alan and Milton got along so well but they genuinely seemed to like each other and Milton deferred to Alan on technical decisions.

Rumors of the Demise of Whitespace Time

Over the next year, Patty was almost completely heads-down working on the mobile integration. Other members of the Whitespace Time task force were similarly busy with their own assignments. As a result, nobody picked up the ball to organize the quarterly Hack Days. Two quarters went by without one.

Boris reached out to Patty to ask to meet. When he showed up at her office, he asked "Do you mind if we go for a walk?" It was a nice summer day so a walk sounded like a nice idea. Also, obviously Boris had something on his mind he didn't want to discuss in the office.

After some pleasantries and asking about each other's work, Patty cut to the chase. "So what's up Boris?"

"I'm bummed that after all the work we've done, Whitespace Time is now dead!"

"Dead? Whitespace Time is not dead! Remember, Noel said it was for everyone. I haven't heard him take it back."

"Sure, officially in Noel's mind Whitespace Time exists. But ever since the layoffs, managers haven't been allowing their employees to use it."

Patty thought about her conversation with Milton. It was true she hadn't had much luck getting the Mobile Division to use Whitespace Time. She had just assumed it was only a problem in her group.

Boris continued. "It doesn't help that we've stopped Hack Days. Ask any employee and they'll tell you that Whitespace Time is no longer supported."

"Boris, you're certainly making good points but people only think Whitespace Time is no longer supported because nobody is spending time organizing and educating. Maybe we need to get the old gang back together."

"I don't know Patty. The mood has changed at Prizmic. I don't know if leadership will want us to spend our time that way."

"I think they will. I mean, I'm sure Noel will want us to. Tell you what — let's set up time to meet with him and see what he says."

"Do you think he'll have time to meet with us?"

"We won't know if we don't ask."

The Mandate

Two weeks later Patty, Boris, and Derwin (who had been roped in) met with Noel. They laid out the case. After the layoffs, managers were no longer supporting Whitespace Time. Most employees thought it was dead. They needed a mandate from him so they can spend time reenergizing Whitespace Time.

Noel listened patiently. Then he asked. "How many employees are using Whitespace Time? What are they telling you the barriers are? What are the managers telling you on why they are no longer supporting it?"

Patty had a pained expression on her face. Noel was asking reasonable questions. But they had showed up to the meeting with no data to back what they were saying. "Oh man," she thought to herself, "I bet he's going to light into us now."

Noel continued. "Have you run a survey or collected any information?"

"No we haven't" said Patty, her head visibly lowered.

"If you want to drive a change initiative, it's important to have data as your burning platform. Also, if you want people to respond to you, it's important that they feel their voices have been heard. Ask them what challenges they're experiencing using Whitespace Time. If you run a survey and conduct interviews, when you present your recommendation, you can start by saying 'Here's what we heard from you.' Then they'll be more receptive to what you have to say. Do you think you can do that?"

Patty was relieved. Rather than scolding them, Noel was instead coaching them on how to move forward.

"Yes, we can do that!" said Patty, with a smile.

"Good! I'd also like to know how other companies manage their Whitespace Time programs. It always helps to have benchmarks.

"Also, make time to talk to each member of my staff to find out how they are thinking about Whitespace Time. When you have a recommendation, I want you to run it by them first and hear their concerns before you bring it to me."

After the trio left the CEO's office, Boris said: "What the heck just happened?"

Patty said, "He's given us a bunch of work to do!"

"I know, but that's not what we wanted! Why couldn't he just give us the mandate we asked for?"

Derwin shook his head. "Because if we're going to drive lasting cultural change, we can't rely on a mandate. That might work for a short time but we'll eventually end up in square one again."

"Yes," Patty said. "Driving culture change is much harder work."

Collecting Information to Make Their Case

The first order of business was learning how other companies were running their employee autonomy programs. Derwin was good friends with a PM at Google who could share how Google ran their 20% Time Program. Derwin found out that Google had a dedicated Google Labs team. His biggest takeaway from what Google was doing that Prizmic was having dedicated staff to manage the program who had a charter to make it easier for employees to share their projects with customers.

The second order of business was creating an employee survey to find out how many employees were using Whitespace Time. Derwin took the action item to design the survey which the task force would review and give feedback on. He used Google Forms which made distributing the survey and collating results easy so that most of his work was in crafting the right questions.

The survey included the questions "Over the past six months, how often did you use Whitespace Time?" with a response scale from "Less than 10 hours" (which the team would consider non-use) to "Over 40 hours" (full use). The survey also probed on how satisfied employees were with the Whitespace Time program, and whether there were barriers to adoption. **[See Key Resource: The Whitespace Time Survey]**[1]

A week later, the survey was sent out to all employees across the company and the response was brisk. After the first day, they already had responses from over 200 employees. Many of the responses were exactly what was expected. Whitespace Time utilization was low (only 8%). Many employees indicated that their managers weren't allowing them to use it. But a big surprise was a couple of the biggest reasons given for not using Whitespace Time were "I didn't know about Whitespace Time" and "I don't know how

---

[1] Page 205

to use it." The survey had indeed provided the burning platform that the team expected but they also learned a few surprises.

Vikram Agrawal, the architect who had been part of the team to win the first Hack Day grand prize came by to see Patty. "I saw the employee survey you guys sent out on Whitespace Time."

"Great!" Patty said. "What do you think?"

"I think you guys are wasting your time! You should kill the program!"

Patty was shocked. Given Vikram had won a Hack Day grand prize, she assumed he would be a big fan of Whitespace Time and would want it to continue. "Why do you say that?"

"It's a useless program. It supposedly gives us time to innovate but the company doesn't care about our projects which end up going nowhere!"

"What about your PPP project? You won the grand prize!"

"That's exactly what I'm talking about! I didn't care about the prize. I wanted PPP to become a funded project. Even though we got it working and made changes based on the feedback we received, no manager wanted to take it forward."

"Has your team stopped working on it?"

"Yes! A project can't stay as a Whitespace Time project forever. The team got tired and even their managers suggested they move on to something else."

"Well I don't think we should throw the baby out with the bathwater. Remember Voice-It succeeded?" Voice-It was Whitespace Time's flagship success project and Patty would often refer to it.

"I don't know how those guys were able to convince management but I've been completely flummoxed. If you're going to continue the program, you need to find a way to make it easier for teams to get funding."

Patty was troubled by her conversation with Vikram. It was a harsh reality check to have someone like him be such a passionate detractor of Whitespace Time. She realized she'd need to spend a lot more time making the program better and more sustainable.

The Rounds

The bad news wasn't over for Patty. After the survey came making the rounds talking individually to each member of CEO Noel Spence's staff. It had only been two years since Noel had declared Whitespace Time for everyone. Yet in time elapsed, that message had been drowned out by other priorities. It seemed not everyone had truly bought into Whitespace Time. While Dan Lewinsky, the GM of the Consumer Division was still a strong supporter, the other executives were more circumspect.Patty already knew what Milton, GM of the Mobile Division thought so she decided to skip having that meeting.

The VP of HR, Harriet Ingram and the Chief Legal Counsel, Olivia Chen were both supportive but said their employees would need help on how to effectively use Whitespace Time.

Janice Hult, the VP of Customer Support, had harder pushback. "My employees are hourly workers. I don't know what it means to give them 10% of their time to work on their ideas. I don't even know if they have any decent ideas! Who's going to pay for them to play around?"

In the case of the Enterprise Division, the former GM Lindsey Badal had left Prizmic six months prior to take another job in Washington State. The new GM, Walter Hicks was completely unaware of the Whitespace Time program. "Help me understand why we would give employees time to do what they want?" he asked.

Patty unintentionally but very visibly sighed before responding. She was remembering her difficult conversation with Milton. She gave her standard employee engagement explanation but Walter didn't seem convinced.

"Have ANY successful projects come out of Whitespace Time?" he asked.

"Oh yes, we've had several. The one we talk about the most is Voice-It," Patty said. She proceeded to share the VP of Sales estimate that it had driven 30% of sales growth that year.

"Wow! That's amazing!" said Walter. "Why didn't you tell me that first? Growth is the biggest challenge we face and if Whitespace Time drives growth, you should lead with that!"

The CIO, Randy Mercer, thought Whitespace Time was a good program for the business units but didn't see how it would help his organization. VP of Sales Rafael Hernandez had similar thoughts. Patty explained to each of them that employees could work on process improvements and internal tools to improve efficiency.

The last executive Patty met with was CTO Sebastian Veksler. Sebastian was more than just supportive. He wanted to help drive forward the proposal.

"I wish you guys had come to me sooner. You've done some really great work and it's a shame we regressed so much over the last year. What are you thinking of proposing?"

"Well, I think we should plan on running the survey regularly so we're constantly on top of the utilization numbers. Also we should bring back Hack Days. Oh, we also should have someone help people on groups like Sales, HR, and Legal learn how to use Whitespace Time effectively," Patty said.

"What else have you learned?"

"Well employee engagement is not the only benefit of Whitespace Time. In fact, there are many other benefits and perhaps the most important is that it helps drive growth."

"That's an important point. It probably didn't help the program that employee engagement was no longer a top priority during the downturn. I'd love to see in your proposal all the benefits of Whitespace Time. Make the case for it as bulletproof as possible!"

"I agree. There were plenty of bullets coming my way during the rounds with the executives!""

Ha ha! Don't worry. They have the best of intentions and only want what's best for Prizmic. Anything else?"

"Oh yes, this is important. We'll need a dedicated team. The challenge to sustain the program is hard enough already but expecting it to happen as a few people's side jobs makes it downright impossible. Google has a Google Labs team dedicated to their 20% time program. We should assemble a similar team."

"Who do you suppose will manage that team?" asked Sebastian.

"I'm not sure, I haven't thought a lot about it. Perhaps a program manager?"

"Will a program manager be able to help the functions learn how to use Whitespace Time?"

"I guess a program manager with experience leading innovation."

"But how much influence will they have with our engineering groups. Shouldn't it be someone very familiar with our product development process?"

"I suppose…" Patty said.

"If only there was someone we knew who was passionate about this program, understood innovation, and knew the company well."

Sebastian was smiling but Patty didn't know why yet.

The Second Time Around

Four weeks later, Patty, Boris, and Derwin presented their proposal at the CEO's staff meeting with Sebastian as their sponsor. **[See Key Resource: The Whitespace Catalysts Proposal]**[1]. As Sebastian had suggested, they

---

[1] Page 214

spent a lot of time documenting the benefits of the program.

They also thought about what the keys were to making it sustainable. How do they ensure managers continue to support employees having time to work on their own ideas? How do they make sure enthusiastic employees don't become disgruntled like Viram? These were all elements they tackled in the proposal including establishing a new Whitespace Catalysts team that would report to Sebastian.

Most of the staff was very supportive, although Milton and Janice were noticeably quiet. It turned out with Milton's lock-up period from the Makeni acquisition had recently expired and would announce his resignation a few weeks later. Janice, on the other hand, seemed to be astutely political and didn't want to be the lone naysayer.

Randy remarked "I'm looking forward to learning how to make this work in my organization. I talked to a few of my managers and they told me so many of our people have tons of great ideas but no way to put them into action."

Patty was pleased to see Randy was now firmly a supporter of the program.

Harriet spoke up. "I've already told Patty that I like the proposal but we'll need help making it work in HR."

Janice finally said something. "Yes, that's right. We need to figure out how to make it work for non-salaried employees as well." That was a close as she would get to objecting.

Noel concluded the discussion. "OK, let's move forward with this proposal. Sebastian, do you have an idea of who will lead this team?"

"As a matter of fact, I do!"

Commentary: It Must Be Somebody's Day Job

Companies shouldn't expect to drive growth via innovation for free.
Sure, some wonderful things in life like hugs, smiles, and love are
free. But highly skilled labor that generates new levels of delight for
customers? Nope, not for free, no you don't.

And when a company first spins up a new capability, say an innovation
program, the tendency is to think that flywheel will keep spinning,
strongly, for all eternity. With no maintenance. Keeping that flywheel
spinning is definitely not free.

Prizmic, like every other company, must continuously nurture its culture.
The culture of innovation the team has begun to build needs stewards,
curators, and drivers.

In growing the innovation culture, Google is an especially interesting
case. Almost from its inception in 1998, Google encouraged employees
to "spend 20% of their time working on what they think will most
benefit Google." Even with big successes from 20% time like AdSense
and Gmail, Google found that just declaring the policy wasn't enough.
Too many employees found it too hard to fit in their 20% projects
around their assigned work. This challenge led to a group of volunteers
who dubbed themselves "Inter-Grouplets" who used their 20% time to
make it easier for other employees to use their 20% time. By 2009, this
volunteer effort had became formalized.

The new Google Labs team had the full time jobs of nurturing and
driving the 20% time program and related avenues like the Google Labs
experimentation system.

The Google Labs team worked to enable testing and release of
incubative new concepts developed by Google employees. The efforts
resulted in hundreds of experiments. These experiments led to some of
Google's largest advances—Gmail, Adsense (pre-dates Google Labs but
came from 20% time), Google Now, Android watch, Mobile platform

advances, etc.—driving roughly 50% of Google's current revenue.

Steve Blank, author of "4 Steps to the Epiphany" points out that companies wishing to innovate well increasingly realize they need a central "innovation capability." Firms like Coca Cola, SAP, Fisher Investments, Clif Bar, Netflix, NASA, Steelcase, Kimberly Clark, Anheuser Busch, and Tivo all have a VP of Innovation, with a team, to drive capability across the organization.

Blank observes that these companies then initiate and continuously improve a system of "trickle up innovation." These medium and large companies enable entrepreneurial small teams to operate as a swarm of customer-focused virtual startups, all aligned to corporate goals.[8] The "trickle up" is not some form of entropic evaporation. Rather, employee's ideas and project teams climb a veritable beanstalk connected up to the company's mission and vision.

This trickle up innovation model is of course a play on words in relationship to the well-known "Trickle up economics" theory described by economist John Maynard Keynes. But Blank isn't talking about that economic theory, rather he is using the metaphor to describe how innovative ideas and behaviors can move up from the bottom of an organization to become the key innovations that drive growth. Blank's trickle up approach requires a corporate environment that first informs all employees about top strategic priorities. Then employees are allowed to get outside the building, learn from customers, experiment with ideas, collect evidence of "what actually works in the real world", and present that evidence to leaders looking to make evidence-based decisions.

But Blank knows this "trickle friendly" corporate environment doesn't just organically appear. The function he calls the "VP of Innovation" actively lays the groundwork to keep the trickle from becoming a dry river bed.

GOOGLE LABS KEY PRINCIPLES

While figuring out how to enable 20% time teams to make fast progress, the Google Labs team developed a set of key principles useful to any team driving innovation.

It really does take a team. David Sedano recruited Mamie Rheingold to join the Google Labs staff to help drive Google Labs and ensure that the innovation needs of employees were established and protected. With team members Pablo Cohn, Arthur Gleckler, and Ricardo Jenez already on board, they were able to commit to continuously improving the innovation culture and methodology available to employees.

The path to experimentation must to be low-friction. The team found that approval for experimentation was a horrible boat anchor. Instead, they instilled a process where any Google employee could run an experiment after passing a set of Labs checks and guidelines. Gatekeeping was of course important since a large public company can be sued, customer data could be compromised, the brand could be hurt, and experiments could bring down the data center. But the Labs team established checks and guidelines that both protected Google and the innovation capability of employees.

Space matters. Of the many Labs experiments, the "Garage," a collaborative workspace that 20% time teams could "rent out," was one of the most successful. By setting up available space for teams to work, flexible seating, and access to materials helpful for rapid prototyping with customers, the Garage was (and still is) a favorite with Google employees.

Connections matter. Mamie teamed up with David Sedano in 2010 to find out why people were not using their 20% time. They found that 20% time innovators were having trouble finding teammates. Collaboration needed some orchestration! So Mamie and team formed an "open marketplace" for 20% time projects. Soon employees were finding, and teaming-up with, colleagues with common interests.

Keep Experimenting. The team found that to improve, Google Labs itself needed to run experiments. Just like the "I can't find teammates" problem was identified and solved, the Labs team discovered and addressed a large list of issues. As one example: Innovators were having trouble making progress. So Labs started a "Pool Your Time" program where employees saved up to work a whole week instead of just one day a week. Then the "pooled time" teams would sprint from Idea-to-Demo in five days.

De-risking as a way of life. One obstacle loomed larger than others: Some employees seemed resistant to, almost afraid of, Google Labs. So the Labs team went to each of the eight gatekeepers (key Google employees tasked with approving what software deployed through each channel) and asked, what are you scared of?

The answer became clear: Labs could bring down the whole Google Front End. After discussion they came to an agreement. The Google App Engine was designed to make writing and testing new software easier and safer. So if Google Labs agreed to have all their experiments built on the App Engine, the Gatekeepers would agree to an expedited approval process for Labs apps.

So a new policy emerged: if you agree to conform to a set of guidelines, the default answer to releasing your experiment would be: "fine, you can release this experiment without any explicit permission." Specifically, if you wrote your software using the App Engine, released internally first, and gave 7 days notice before release, you would be in conformance. The Google team called this system "The Flagline." When an experiment and experimenter were in conformance with guidelines, they were considered "on the Flagline."

Experiments that wanted to deviate from the Flagline were required to request explicit approval from relevant system "gatekeepers" who understood both the relevant software systems and the goals of the experiment. It wasn't impossible to release an experiment not built on Google App Engine, just more difficult. If no gatekeepers objected to the "non Flagline" experiment, the experiment was allowed to go live.

To offer peace of mind Google-wide, experiments could be taken down by anyone, in any functional group within Google. If anything at all looked suspicious, any Googler could hit a big red button and take the app down. Risk mitigated.

In this way, Google Labs enabled smart, and careful, empowerment. Using this methodology for releasing experiments with a minimum of resistance, the Google Labs team established a string of wins and key innovation principles that help to propel Google forward today.

THE CHANGE

In July 2011, when Larry Page took over from Eric Schmidt as Google CEO, one of his first decisions was to "put more wood behind fewer arrows" by canceling numerous projects. One of the casualties was the Google Labs team, in spite of newer successes like Google Now and the Android watch. Since 2011, there have been a number of blogs and press reports claiming Google no longer supports 20% time. But the spirit of Google Labs was not dead. Page indicated that the work of the Labs team would continue inside individual product organizations. One of Google Labs creations, "The Garage," continues to run as of 2016.

Google's shutting down the Labs team is not an indictment of the 20% time approach. When reporters and lay people alike dig a little deeper, it's clear the 20% time program still exists. But it also seems clear that no longer having the team in place to advocate-for and enable 20% time has taken a toll. Reports from inside "the Googleplex" vary, but rumors have it that the program lacks the same level of nurturing it formerly had. The lesson is clear: if you want to drive innovation inside your company, have a dedicated team to support it.

Prizmic has started by establishing the job title "Innovation Leader" and identifying an employee whose full-time job is to nurture and grow the innovation culture. **[See Resource: Innovation Leader Job Description]**[1]

---

[1] Page 228

The Offer

After the CEO staff meeting, Sebastian asked Patty to come to his office. To her surprise, her current manager Alan Overfield was waiting for them there.

"Uh, what's going on?" Patty asked.

Sebastian closed the door. "Patty, we would like to promote you to Director of Innovation reporting to me. Alan is here to tell you he supports you making this change."

"Absolutely!" Alan said. "You have done some amazing work in your career at Prizmic but your work on Whitespace Time has made the biggest impact on the company. I can't think of anyone better to lead innovation at Prizmic."

Patty was genuinely surprised but as it sank in realized that she should have seen it coming. "But I'm an engineer. I've never managed a team!"

"Don't sell yourself short. You have led bigger initiatives than most managers. When it comes to innovation, you have instant credibility and many employees will happily take your lead. Your work with the task force is testament to that."

"Thank you. This is a great honor. Please can I have time to think about it?"

"Of course," replied Sebastian. "Here's the formal offer letter. Take a few days and let us know."

As soon as Patty left Sebastian's office, she called her husband Rick. "You won't believe what happened!" She told him about the offer.

"So how much more are you going to be making?" he asked.

"I didn't even look!" She unfolded the offer letter. "Oh wow!" The bump in compensation was much bigger than she expected.

"So you already accepted, right?" Rick said.

"No, I asked for time to think about it."

"You're kidding me! This is your dream job. You better take it before they change their minds!"

"What do you mean it's my dream job? I've alway seen myself as an engineer"

"No, I've been watching you. You were most happy when you were working on that task force. You haven't been as into work with this mobile stuff you've been doing."

Patty hadn't realized that about herself so Rick's observation was a revelation. It made sense that for her own personal growth, she should make the change. She remembered Rowan's advice to step out of her comfort zone.

"This is so cool! Are you going to buy me a BMW to celebrate?" Rick said.

"Not a chance!"

The next day after she accepted the offer, Patty called up her former boss Rowan.

"Congratulations Patty! That's awesome news. I know you'll be great."

"Do you have any advice for me?"

"You're smart and I know you'll figure things out. Just don't get too comfortable. Keep questioning everything you're doing and find ways to improve. You won't always have supportive leaders so your best defense will be having a compelling track record of success and presenting it well."

Her Whitespace Time collaborators were very excited for Patty. Boris organized an impromptu congratulations lunch. "You're going to pay for the bill," Boris said looking her straight in the eye. "I'm not kidding!"

At the lunch, Pankaj Aron, who had been at the very first task force meeting, leaned over to Patty. "When you start hiring your team, please make space for me." Patty felt flattered. Pankaj was a great engineer and it would be an honor to have him on her team.

Boris who overhead jumped in: "Not before she hires me!"

Conclusion

Your intrapreneurs are your key asset, your future. To unleash the power of these employees, give them the support they need and deserve. This is the configuration you need: All employees are supported by a central, internal team of innovation coaches who provide the tools, mindset and guidance needed to accelerate innovative progress. These dedicated 'capability builders' will become powerful tuners and amplifiers for your thriving culture of intrapreneurship.

CHAPTER 4
DEPLOYING DESIGN THINKING

"Design is not just what it looks like and feels like. Design is how it works."
- Steve Jobs

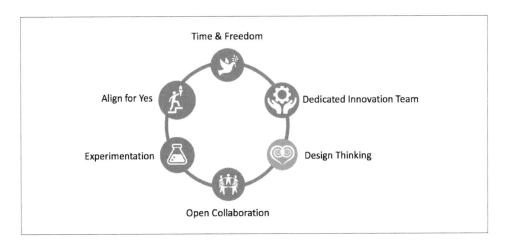

Introduction

Anyone can be a successful intrapreneur. To successfully create a culture where everyone innovates, you must equip your employees with Design Thinking skills. Then every employee, whether they work in HR, IT, Product, Legal or Finance, can be an intrapreneur. And effective intrapreneurs can solve tough business problems.

This is because Design Thinking helps your intrapreneurs to focus on developing innovative solutions that match customer needs. Design Thinking guides both the "what will constitute a good target for innovation", as well as the "how to effectively innovate". Without Design Thinking human nature tends to take over, and us humans dive straight into our own opinions, and quickly fall in love with our own opinions and solutions. Sometimes this works, but for the most part, the highly opinionated, solution-back thought process generates lots of expensive solutions to problems that may not even truly exist.

When companies figure out how to infuse their culture with Design Thinking, employees focus on customer needs, innovate with speed and a precise attention to learning from customers as they go, and therefore drive better business results.

Forming the Team

Patty, Alan, and Sebastian knew this was a new phase for Whitespace Time. With dedicated resources assigned to nurturing Whitespace Time, there would be a higher level of scrutiny and expectations. Patty and her team would need to be much more methodical in their approach. Patty, Alan, and Sebastian agreed on a six week transition period to hand off her Mobile Division tasks and ramp up to her new innovation leader role. Sebastian and Patty had weekly 1-on-1 meetings. Sebastian knew she would need help adjusting to her new role.

"So have you thought about what your Key Performance Indicators will be for your team?" he asked. Prizmic used Key Performance Indicators (KPIs) as a tool to measure how each team was performing against measurable goals that laddered up to the company's key objectives.

"Well, we want employees to use Whitespace Time, so that could be one. But I don't know if measuring utilization is enough. People might perceive us as just rewarding activity instead of results."

"I agree. It would be much better if you can think of KPIs that tie more directly to business goals. In your Whitespace Time pitch, you talk about growth. Is there any way we can capture that?"

"I suppose we can measure how many Whitespace projects graduate and become formally funded projects."

"I like that! The fact that the project graduated means some leader with budget thought enough of the project that they allocated scarce dollars to it."

"We can call that KPI the 'Number of Whitespace Graduates,'" Patty suggested.

"Great! How many Graduates do you think you can have in the first year?"

"Well, we're not just counting new products. New features count. Process improvements and internal tools. I think we can easily do 25."

"I agree, 25 would be easy. You should set the goal to 50!"

Patty swallowed hard. "I guess this is what it feels to not be in the comfort zone!" she thought to herself.

Sebastian smiled as he noticed Patty's unease. "Look, I think it's important that your goals are very aspirational. I suggest you go back, think about it, and work with your new team on a complete set of KPIs."

"Me and my big mouth," Patty thought to herself later. "How am I going to get 50 Graduates in a year?"

She urgently needed to put a team into place. The first order of business would be to get Hack Days going again and she knew just the right people to make it happen. Sebastian had only agreed to give her two headcount to start with the possibility to grow the team later.

Boris was an obvious choice. He was just as passionate about Whitespace Time as she was and he was fun to work with. People enjoyed his sense of humor. Even though Pankaj had already volunteered, Patty wasn't sure how she would use an engineer. She needed someone to help organize and train. It made sense to ask Derwin.

"I appreciate the offer Patty but I don't want to be on an innovation team," Derwin explained. "I'm a product manager and that job has a clear growth path. I'm not sure what will happen to my career if I come and work for you."

Patty tried to object. Wasn't it more important to do something you're passionate about? But she couldn't refute his main thesis that the work that they were doing had an uncertain career path.

"Besides," Derwin added, "I think I'll be more help to you if I stay in this job. You're going to need champions in every division and every function. You won't have a more eager champion than me!"

Derwin's words resonated.

Given the tiny size of her team, Patty would need to work in a highly leveraged way. She made a note to organize a community of Whitespace Time Champions. The champions would not be formally part of her team but employees who enthusiastically supported Whitespace Time.

The Designer

Carol Jacobs, a user-interface designer from the Enterprise Division had reached out to Patty for a meeting. Patty didn't know Carol, who at eleven months of tenure was relatively new to Prizmic.

Carol quickly cut to the chase: "I heard you'll be leading an innovation team for Prizmic. I wanted to let you know that I'd love to join you."

"Thanks so much for your reaching out," Patty said. "Please tell me why you're interested."

"Well are you familiar with 'design thinking'?"

"A little bit. I've heard of it," Patty said.

"I learned design thinking at the Stanford Design School and used to teach workshops at my previous company. I truly believe we can make Whitespace Time much more effective if we teach employees to use design thinking on their projects."

Patty was intrigued. "Tell me how that would work."

"Here's one example. When human beings are faced with a problem, they fall in love with the very first idea that comes to mind. It turns out the first idea we think of is almost always not the best. It's much better to think of lots and lots of possible ideas to curate the best one. We can teach employees to come up with lots of possible solutions to the problem they're trying to solve."

What Carol was saying made sense to Patty. It was also becoming clear that having an expert in design thinking on her team would be a critical asset especially with groups like HR and Legal that didn't think of themselves as innovators. Patty had found her second team member. Actually, the second team member had found her.

Commentary: Design Thinking

IDEO CEO Tim Brown defines Design thinking as "a human-centered approach to innovation that draws from the designer's toolkit to integrate the needs of people, the possibilities of technology, and the requirements for business success". By "thinking like a designer", Design Thinking methods have proved to be effective at delivering effective results across a wide range of business areas.

Intuit has distilled Design Thinking into three principles they collectively call "Design for Delight" (D4D). The three principles are **Deep Customer Empathy**, **Go Broad To Go Narrow**, and **Rapid Experimentation With Customers**.

Design for Delight

Deep Customer Empathy

In Design Thinking, we attempt to understand the customer better than they understand themselves. This requires the discipline to set aside our own opinions and observe customers performing tasks in their own natural environments. To fully uncover a customer's motivations, we not only capture what they do and say, we also want to try to capture what they are thinking and feeling (see the Customer Empathy Map).

The Customer Empathy Map

Go Broad To Go Narrow

In human nature, when faced with a problem, we tend to fall in love with the very first solution that comes to mind. Studies have shown that it's very unlikely that the first solution that occurs to us will be the best solution and it's best to go for quantity of ideas first (Osborn, A.F. (1963) Applied imagination: Principles and procedures of creative problem solving (Third Revised Edition). New York, NY: Charles Scribner's Sons). Going Broad To Go Narrow imposes the discipline of creating options before making choices. Often the best idea will surface after dozens of other ideas or it may be an amalgamation of several ideas.

For innovation, one effective tool we've used for going broad before narrowing is the 7-to-1 methodology. In this approach, each member of the team is tasked with separately coming up with seven different ways of solving a particular problem. We've found that coming up with the first three or four ideas for each individual is pretty easy. After that, individuals are forced to think outside of the box to come up with more options. Frequently, the very best ideas are these non-obvious ones. When the team comes together to share out their 7-to-1 assignments, there's further room for ideation by combining and building upon the best elements of ideas shared.

Rapid Experimentation With Customers

Rather than attempting to implement a perfect plan in a waterfall approach, Design Thinking dictates that you accept that your ideas will be fundamentally flawed at the start and that getting to a delightful product requires rapid experiments with customers and learning how to make the product better. In this case, the Rapid Experimentation With Customers completely aligns with the goals and practices of the Lean Startup Methodology.

Examples

Design thinking works. For example, Bank of America's Keep the Change Program was born of Design Thinking.

Customers would have never said "hey, I want a debit card that will 'keep the change' for me."

They just wouldn't think of it. But IDEO -- brought in to help Bank of America try Design Thinking -- observed people rounding up to the next dollar when paying for things. So what if that habit were combined with a debit card making an easy, frictionless way to save possible?

The team started with a customer observation, ideated some possible ways to put that to use, and then arrived at something people really wanted to do. Automatically, seamlessly storing away that virtual change which would have lived surrounding by tiny lint-balls, deep in pockets, is that useful? Sure, why not?

As a result, Bank of America has gotten 10 million new customers and $1.8 billion in savings for those people using "keep the change" debit cards. The bank was so happy with the results they've shared some of the wealth, matching the first $400 placed in each new savings account.

And Design Thinking is not only for products. Many organizations have found that Design Thinking creates breakthroughs in process innovation. Kaiser Permanente for example, used Design Thinking to reimagine how both productivity and quality of care could improve. The major data around problems across nursing shift changes drove focus on those points in time. Shift changing overlaps took 40 minutes. And a multitude of errors occurred across too many transfers of information.

Kaiser Permanente employees, their Design Thinking Intrapreneurs, studied how nurses interacted with patients and each other. They observed in practice a number of behaviors that represented key opportunities for improvement. One key opportunity was shift changes: they were slow and left room for errors. They considered a multitude of different possible approaches, ran experiments, and landed on some new shift change principles and a new process. The results were amazing. The new shift change process cut the time from 40 minutes to 12. Even more critically, the team reduced errors during information transfer, thereby increasing patient confidence.

New Hire Orientation

The very next day after her first team meeting, Patty bumped into the VP of HR Harriet Ingram in the office kitchen.

"Hi Patty, I'm glad to run into you," Harriet started. "I've been thinking about how my organization can take advantage of Whitespace Time. Our customers are usually our fellow employees."

"That's right," Patty said. "Internal process improvements make for good Whitespace projects."

"I'm happy you said that—that's what I've been trying to encourage my team to think about. In particular, one of my pet peeves for a while now has been our new hire orientation. Nobody in the company thinks we do a particularly good job of onboarding new employees and yet nothing we've tried seems to have made a difference and we've tried a lot!"

"Yes, my employee orientation was years ago but I do remember still feeling lost after it was done."

"Exactly! I have a couple of HR Specialists who are passionate about this problem. However, they don't consider themselves very innovative. I was wondering if your team could help them?"

"Why certainly!" Patty replied. She immediately thought of Carol and thought this would be a good assignment for her to use her design thinking skills.

"Wonderful!" Harriet said with a big smile. "I'll have Natalia and Essam reach out to you."

Carol was excited to get the assignment to help the HR Specialists. When they met, she described the philosophy of design thinking. "The first thing we want to do is get deep customer empathy. We want to understand our customers, in this case, the new hires, better than they understand themselves. Then based on the insights we gather, we want to come up with as many ideas as we can before we choose what idea to work on. Finally, we'll run quick experiments to see how well our idea works. We'll keep experimenting until we get it right."

"How do we get to understand customers better than they understand themselves? That doesn't even sound possible," Essam asked.

"Well if we could literally walk in their shoes, that would be ideal. But the next best thing is to observe them. We want to gather what they say, what they do, what they're thinking and what they're feeling."

"How do you know what someone is thinking and feeling?" Natalia asked.

"Good question. For what their thinking, we have to ask unless either of you is a mind reader!" That elicited some chuckles. "For what they're feeling, we can often observe from their facial expressions or body language. We can also ask them that too."

"This sounds great! I want to try. How are we going to go about observing the new hires?" Natalia asked.

"I suggest we participate in a new hire orientation as if we were new hires ourselves," Carol said. "Not only will we be able to observe the new hires, but we'll be able to feel what it's like from their perspective."

The Prizmic new hire orientation was held every other Monday and ran from 9 am in the morning through lunch. During that time, new hires would fill in HR paperwork, watch a company overview presentation, be welcomed by a senior leader, receive an explanation of benefits, be taken on a tour of the campus, and finally have lunch with their assigned mentor from the team they were joining.

Carol, Essam, and Natalia attended the next orientation incognito. For the most part, they were quiet observers. Right before lunch, they used a fifteen minute break to ask the group of new hires questions about what they had experienced. They also had every new hire fill in a Net Promoter Survey survey about their new hire experience.

In their meeting that afternoon, Essam and Natalia were bursting with ideas and were eager to start brainstorming. Among the dozens of solutions they came up with included content the new hires wanted but was missing ("how do I make friends?"; "how do I find people to carpool with"), parts they found tedious (filling out HR forms), and parts that were too brief (the senior leader welcome).

After an affinity exercise where similar ideas were grouped, Essam and Natalia voted and chose as their first solution introducing online documents for employees to sign before their hire date. That solution was deployed in the next orientation and the Net Promoter Survey, although not scientific, seemed to confirm that it had improved the experience. Essam and Natalia now had the confidence to try out other ideas on their own.

Many weeks later, Natalia and Essam brought Carol a bottle of wine to thank her for her help. Carol asked how the new hire orientation improvements were going.

"It's been wonderful. We've made huge improvements!" Natalia said.

"That's great! What's made the biggest difference?" Carol asked.

"Interesting, it was something not very obvious. It turned out the biggest pain new hires experience is configuring their new computer and getting all their Prizmic server accounts set up. It can take over a week for an employee to get all their issues resolved."

"That makes a lot of sense. How did you solve that?"

"We had a couple of technicians from IT deliver the computers to the new hires during orientation and help them with their account setups," Essam replied.

"That's great! Congratulations!"

"Yes, thanks so much for your help. We're getting a lot of recognition in HR for our work. We're having an offsite in a couple of weeks and Harriet wants us to present our design thinking project!"

Carol was excited to later share with Patty and Boris the success of her design thinking coaching with the HR team. Patty was also thrilled. "That was a great outcome with new hire orientation. I especially like how helpful this approach is for employees who don't think of themselves as innovators. How can we scale what you did to other groups?"

"Too bad there's only one of you," Boris said. "Design thinking can turn every Prizmic employee into an innovator."

"I suppose I could offer to teach a workshop…" Carol thought out loud.

"That's a fantastic idea! Why don't you write up a proposal for a design thinking workshop? We can invite a few people to a pilot workshop, and if that goes well, we can decide how often we offer it?"

Carol subsequently developed a "Designing Joy" one-day workshop. **[See Resource: Designing Joy (Design Thinking Workshop)]**[1]. The workshop would prove to be popular and effective and Carol would eventually offer it to Prizmic employees every other month.

---

[1] Page 242

Conclusion

The illiterate of the 21st century will not be those who cannot read and write, but those who cannot learn, unlearn and relearn. – Alvin Toffler

You need your employees to commit to Design Thinking. The most valuable skillset for intrapreneurs is the toolkit that helps them achieve customer obsession, to define and live with the "problem", to rapidly experiment with possible solutions and learn their way to driving customer delight.

Giving employees Design Thinking skills will lead to significant payoffs. But, when rolling out a Design Thinking program, you're sure to encounter pushback from some stakeholders. Change is hard, and some employees and leaders will be concerned that Design Thinking will slow progress, distract people from strategic priorities, defocus the current efforts, and put droves of picky designers in charge of all products. But these concerns are theoretical in nature, and looking at the performance of companies that have strongly supported Design Thinking programs indicates otherwise.

Success stories for corporate Design Thinking programs abound [**See Key Resource: <u>Making the Case for Design Thinking</u>**][1]. So you need to respond to pushback with the powerful stories and data points that illustrate the true value of Design Thinking.

You can take a stepwise approach to bring Design Thinking to your company. The best and most achievable first steps are to find a core set of employees passionate about Design Thinking. These employees will already be highly motivated to help peers become better intrapreneurs. As an example, Intuit decided to focus on Design Thinking, and then over time built up a company-wide team of "Innovation Catalysts". These Innovation Catalysts (ICs) were place into a three levels-deep immersive training program, and asked to spend 10% of their time coaching teams across the company in Design Thinking. Hundreds of employees were trained to become capable of coaching teams in

---

[1] Page 246

Design Thinking. These Innovation Catalysts helped teams understand customers, run experiments, make good decisions, and drive business successes. Over the period of a few years these Innovation Catalysts were able to develop dozens of success stories.

The Innovation Catalyst actions and success stories built credibility, and it became clear that Design Thinking and Innovation Catalysts were helpful to the innovation capability and growth of the company.

If you start with a small core of passionate "would be" Design Thinkers, you can train a growing core of coaches who will spread the wealth. As progress is made, you may then use the success stories and momentum to progress to a scaled set of Design Thinking coaches that operate in all major divisions across your company. For a more detailed view of this approach, see our [**Case Study: "Intuit Innovation Catalysts."**][1]

When you influence your company to move forward with Design Thinking, you will create an environment that is both instructive and supportive for your intrapreneurs. And companies staffed with highly-engaged, Design Thinking, intrapreneurial employees are destined to beat the competition while delighting customers.

[1] Page 254

CHAPTER 5
OPEN COLLABORATION

"No matter who you are,
most of the smartest people work for someone else."
- Bill Joy

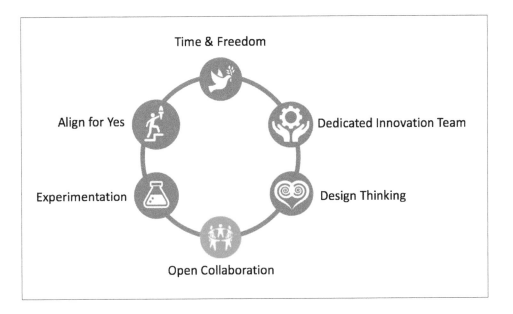

Introduction

Unenlightened managers believe their teams must work in secrecy to protect their ideas from being stolen before they have a chance to succeed. Great leaders understand that ideas without execution have almost no value. They know that working in isolation delays progress and impedes leveraging the work of others. Intrapreneurs must be encouraged to collaborate openly, with employees across organizational and geographic borders, with customers, with vendors, and with partners. You never know who will possess the missing ingredient that will help turn an idea into reality.

Hack Days Redux

Boris was excited about organizing the next Hack Day. "This will be a piece of cake. We've done this so many times already!" Boris took the lead in managing the logistics, getting the word out, and helping teams form and get signed up. The team was able to get most of Noel's CEO staff to volunteer to be judges for the event.

There was one pet peeve Boris wanted to address for the new Hack Days - how employees signed up. The website they had set up for teams to register had proved to be very clunky to navigate. This came up in one of the Whitespace Time Task Force's subsequent meetings. Ilya had noticed that two sets of teams had worked on ideas that were almost identical. "I don't think they would have done that if they knew about each other. In fact, they might have decided to join forces."

"Yes, it would be much better if it was easier to navigate the site to find out what teams were working on, especially if you're looking for a team to join," Boris added.

"Definitely! Remember the designer Dan Sage? He had trouble finding a team even though at least four teams said they needed a designer," Ilya continued. "Teams that are looking for additional team members should be able to indicate that on the site and describe the skills they need."

"That sounds like a really great idea," said Patty. "Not just for Hack Days but for Whitespace Time in general. I'd love for people across the company to know what other teams are working on. We need a more sophisticated idea management tool. Something much better than our clunky website."

"I just did a Google search of 'idea management tools'," Boris said, "and there seems to be a bunch of them. Spigit and Brightidea look like they are among the most popular."

"Do you have time to take a look and evaluate which one would be the best for us?" Patty asked.

"Yes, I'd be happy to. What would you say our requirements are?" Boris asked.

"Easy navigation. Easy to find what teams are working on. Search should work flawlessly," Ilya started.

"We want to encourage feedback and comments. Anybody should be able to give feedback or contribute ideas to a particular project," added Derwin.

"Don't forget a 'Help Wanted' sign so teams can indicate they are looking for more members," added Patty.

"Conversely, individuals should be able to advertise what skills they have to offer," continued Derwin.

"Great! I have easy navigation, feedback, 'Help Wanted', skills. Anything else?" Boris asked.

"A rating system would be helpful," said Ilya.

"Lightweight project management would also be helpful. Something to indicate what status the project is in," said Derwin.

"That's a good list for now," Patty concluded.

Boris ended up recommending Bright Idea. The innovation tool made a positive impact almost right away. There was a Whitespace team in the Enterprise Division that was working on a telephony app. They discovered that another Whitespace team in the Consumer Division had been playing around with VoIP (Voice over IP) technology and had deployed a couple of servers. After reaching out, the Consumer team was happy to let the Enterprise team use their servers which saved the Enterprise team several weeks of effort.

The Task Force loved how for the first time at Prizmic, so many teams were now openly collaborating over organizational and geographic boundaries. The speed of innovation was significantly increased simply because teams were able to find experts and were not wasting time reinventing what somebody else had already done.

Commentary: Selecting an Open Collaboration Tool

You need to put a good collaborative innovation tool in place. These tools generally satisfy two categories of users: employees who manage innovation within the company, and employees who are working on various innovative projects.

Innovators need a few common types of help. They need to form teams, with the innovation system helping them to see which employees out there have relevant skills and interests.

Employees driving innovations need to make fast progress, developing customer empathy, prototyping, running experiments, and building out the new product or service. A powerful open collaboration tool makes previous learning (empathy, experiments, prototypes) visible across the organization. Innovation teams can save tremendous amounts of time by leveraging the lessons, insights and tools other teams have previously developed.

The Innovation Collaboration tool must also help the innovation system leaders curate and communicate projects across the company. So the tool must be visible enterprise-wide, show ideas organized into customer-segment focused lists or "pipelines," and should house all the "Innovation Challenges" that leaders issue to employees. Also important is the ability of the tool to emphasize innovation process steps so employees follow a thoughtful process, including customer research and experimentation. For example, some tools allow the creation of custom-defined milestones or progress check-ins so teams can stay on-track.

The good news is this: A number of vendors, like Crowdicity, Bright Idea and Spigot, to name a few, ship products that largely satisfy these requirements.

Move your company away from stone axes. Your best future lies in using a powerful, open, collaboration-focused innovation tool. Game on!

Where's Everybody?

On the day of the event, there was a noticeable drop in attendance from the previous Hack Day. Patty asked Boris about it. "Where's everybody? I'd estimate there's only two-thirds of the people we got last time."

Boris was a little defensive. "I really worked hard on getting the word out. Maybe we just chose a bad time of year."

"Hmm, when would be a better time of year?" Patty said.

Consumer Division GM Dan Lewinsky came by early to see how teams were doing. He spent an hour floating between teams asking them about their projects. He then called Patty over and asked her discretely: "I saw a few great projects but I must tell you. The event doesn't have the same energy we've seen in the past."

"I'm afraid you might be right. We don't have the same number of people as before."

"Well maybe you'll just have to work to get the momentum you had before," Dan said.

Patty also floated between teams to see what people were working on. She was glad to see an old friend, software engineer Ilya Smirnov. "Hi Ilya, what are you working on?"

"My idea is a mobile app that uses geo-location to alert you when you're nearby a client's address. I want to add this app to our productivity suite."

"That sounds great. I look forward to playing around with the prototype," said Patty enthusiastically.

"Oh no! I'm not building a prototype. I'm just going to describe the idea the best I can with slides."

"You're breaking my heart Ilya! Why would you just put together slides when you're such an awesome engineer. Surely a prototype is more compelling than slides?!"

"That's what I thought. The last couple of Hack Days, I built prototypes but didn't win. I don't think the judges fully understood the value of the prototype. This time I want to win and having impressive slides that the judges will understand is the way to do it!"

"Um okay," Patty said as she walked away. She was disappointed that one of Prizmic's best engineers had decided the only way to win was to make slides.

As before, the pitch-outs started at 4 pm. This time, there was a lot of confusion. Three different judges rushed over to Patty before the first team pitched:

"I don't understand the judging criteria!"

"How are we supposed to rank teams?"

"What are we supposed to be valuing?"

"This whole thing is badly organized!"

What a contrast from before! In the past, the task force got nothing but love from the leaders for organizing the Hack Days. Now, everyone seemed to be picking on the team for everything that was imperfect.

The teams weren't much happier with the pitching. Each team was limited to two minutes and almost half didn't get to finish. Pankaj Aron, who Patty had asked to reprise his role as timekeeper, was very strict and wouldn't let teams go more than twenty seconds over. One team's prototype crashed as they were trying to demo and when they were cut off for time, they felt their whole day's work was for naught.

And to make matters worse, after the pitch-outs were done, the judges huddled and announced the grand prize winner: Ilya Smirnov's Geo-location Mobile App!

Houston, we have a problem!

Commentary: The Innovation Theater Trap

Hack Days can be an energizing, fun, productive blessing for any company. But they can also be a mess. Companies find lots of ways to get hack days wrong!

For example, don't let your Hack Days become superficial 'beauty contests", where the glossiest hype 'wins'. Hack Days should not enable a shortcut to "winning." You employees to dig in, feel energized, form small teams, and do real innovative work. But the magnetic pull of gloss, hype, powerpoints, and superficial pitching often creeps into the picture.

Leader-judges, quick pitches and winners often become a recipe for disaster. The reason is simple: Humans generally love their own opinions and love energy and excitement. Judging panels can quickly become a cult of strong, opinionated personalities. Just look at Mr. Widerful on Shark Tank! The entertainment values is there, to be sure (it's is a TV show with ratings after all). But to pander to the ego and opinions of judges spells death to true innovation.

So innovation often become a show – and a shallow one at that. The typical issues companies face are:
* Why are the leader's judgments the final say? Aren't those just opinions?
* Do the leader-judges even have the time or background to understand what the innovators did?
* What happens to winning ideas? Do they gain support or are they given a pat on the back and quick brush-off?
* What happens to the crushed spirits of non-winning teams? Maybe one of those non-winning teams was actually onto something really big!
* So as a contestant … why even bother to really innovate?

Given the format, the leader judges, two minute pitches, it's hard to avoid the hype-fest syndrome. Glossy powerpoints, eye-popping videos, and exciting, dramatic presentations upstage all other presentations. The power of customer learning withers. Continuous innovation is replaced with transactional endorphin releases. That's innovation theatre. That's a big step backwards.

The Postpartum

Patty assembled her team the next day for a "postpartum" on the Hack Day. Derwin also joined the discussion.

"Ok, each of you, tell me how you thought the event went?"

Carol started. "That was a lot of fun. It was great to see so many ideas and that senior leaders set aside time for the judging. I think people loved that Dan showed an interest in their projects by spending time with each team."

Boris went next. "I thought it was a big success. Well maybe not a BIG success, but a success. Attendance was a little underwhelming but other than that, I thought it went well."

"What about the feedback from the executives? Did you hear any of that?" Patty asked.

"Oh yes, I heard them whining. They don't appreciate how much work it is to make these events work."

"What about you Derwin?" Patty asked.

"You know, you might be a victim of 'been there, done that.' The Hack Days have lost their novelty factor."

"I think you're onto something Derwin," Patty said.

"What did you think?" Boris asked looking at Patty.

"I thought it wasn't good enough and we need to make dramatic changes." Boris and Carol looked at her in stunned silence. Derwin had a more bemused look on his face and said "Tell us how you really feel Patty!"

"For starters, I think the format of the Hack Days is completely wrong. Perhaps we got away with it in the past because of the novelty factor. But the whole judging process is a fiasco and the criticism we got from the senior leaders was completely valid. But what brought it home for me was having Ilya win the grand prize."

"What was wrong with that?" Boris asked.

"Do you know he told me the way to win was to make slides instead of building a prototype. Instead of doing something truly innovative, he was just playing to win a prize."

"He said that? Oh, that's not good," Carol said.

"Yes he did. Our process rewards projects that present well instead of rewarding work that has the best chance of having an impact. We've got to fix that!" Patty asserted.

"But unless you get rid of prizes, you're always going to need judges," Boris protested.

"Boris, it's not just the judges who were unhappy. A bunch of teams didn't get to finish their pitches and were very disappointed," Patty insisted.

"Yes, two minutes to pitch is a lot of pressure," Carol said. "It would be better if there was more time for questions and answers."

"But the pitch outs would take all day if we gave each team much more time," Boris said.

"Why have pitch outs to begin with? Why not set up a gallery walk where each team has a table. Then the judges could at their leisure visit with each team and spend us much time as they need," Carol suggested.

"Ooh I like that idea," Patty said. "We could open the gallery walk to all employees so participants could show off their projects to a lot more people."

"That does sound better," Boris said. "I could see teams recruiting more members from employees who take an interest in what their doing. That way the work can continue after the Hack Day."

"Good point. I love how a gallery walk also can serve as marketing for Whitespace Time," Patty said.

"I like the gallery walk idea guys, but you still haven't solved the big problem," Derwin said.

"What big problem?" Patty said.

"Look who you have judging. Senior leaders! Why do we assume they can discern what a good idea is?" Derwin said.

"Well, they do have the experience…" Patty started to respond.

Derwin interrupted. "True, they have experience but how relevant is it? I mean, how much time do they actually spend with customers?"

"That's a good point," Carol replied. "A few months ago, the research team organized a series of customer visits and invited employees to sign up. Not a single executive did."

"Ha ha! They are too busy spending all days in meetings with other executives," Boris said.

"Exactly! Isn't it important to have good customer empathy to judge ideas?" Derwin asked. "It just seems senior leaders are likely to overvalue incremental ideas that build on things they are already familiar with."

"You're making a fair point. But if it's not senior leaders, who should we have judge?" Patty said.

"Maybe instead of having senior leader judges, we could have customers attend our Hack Days?" Carol said.

"That's a great idea!" Derwin exclaimed. "The customers could be invited to the gallery walk and they could tell us which products they would actually use!"

"I guess that could work. Actually, I can see how that would be better…"

Boris' mind was obviously chewing on how to change the next Hack Day.

Hack Day With Customers

At the next quarter's Hack Day, Patty and team decided on the theme "How to Better Serve Our Attorney Customers." Attorneys were one of Prizmic's biggest customer verticals and were also their least satisfied group of customers. A focused Hack Day seemed like just the prescription to make significant improvements.

In the weeks ahead of the Hack Day, the team held three info sessions where employees could hear from product managers a prioritized list of feedback they had received from attorneys. The idea was to give teams fodder to chew on for their ideas and make it much more likely that those ideas would align with Prizmic priorities.

On the Hack Day itself, twelve attorneys were invited to participate. The judging panel was eliminated. Instead, at 4 pm, the Hack Day was converted into a gallery walk where the customers and other employees could wander from station to station to see what the Hack Day participants had come up with. Teams were no longer constrained by the two minute pitch-out presentation limit which proved to be a very popular change.

The attorneys were also given $1,000 fake Prizmic Dollars to spend. They were asked to "invest" money in ideas they thought had value and would use in their own practice. They were also encouraged to leave their business cards with teams working on ideas they would be willing to help with by answering the team's questions from time to time. By 6 pm, the Prizmic Dollars were tallied up and the winner identified by having amassed the most money.

At the next postpartum, the team was all smiles having received very positive feedback from Hack Day participants, senior leaders, and maybe most importantly, the attorneys. One attorney even said "This was the most fun I've had in a long time. I wish I could work like this. Maybe I picked the wrong career!"

But the team had learned its lesson well not to rest on its laurels. There were plenty of ideas on how to improve the process going forward.

"A couple of the teams mentioned that their understanding of the customer issues was different from what the product managers had told them after talking to customers," Boris pointed out.

"Yes, it's almost like we would have been better served if we had brought the customers in earlier for the info sessions," Carol said.

"Why don't we do that?" Patty asked.

"Yes we should!" Boris exclaimed. "Instead of hearing from an intermediary, the customers should tell us directly about their pain points."

"Ha ha! We can call that a 'Pain Jam'" Carol laughed.

"'Pain Jam!' I like it," Boris and Patty said in unison.

Conclusion

When intrapreneurs are able to openly collaborate, good things happen. In the open, collaborative environment, ideas flow, teams form, and progress quickens. So great leaders work hard to enable open collaboration. The right tools and mindset allow intrapreneurs to work across geographical and organizational boundaries. A healthy system of collaboration bolsters your innovation culture and interconnects intrapreneurs in ways that accelerate and amplify outcomes.

CHAPTER 6
LEAN EXPERIMENTATION

"In God we trust. All others must bring data."
- W. Edwards Deming

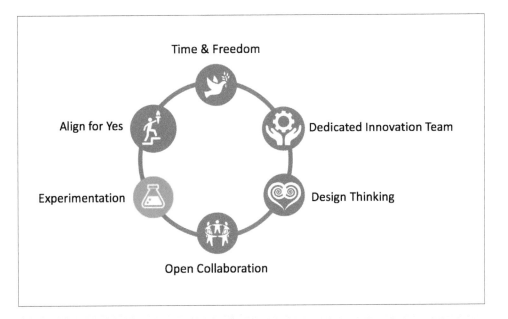

Introduction

The biggest barriers for an employee's great idea coming to fruition are management opinions. Unenlightened managers believe their role is to be the arbiter of ideas by having an opinion on which ideas have value. Great leaders recognize that their opinions are likely to undervalue the most disruptive ideas. These great leaders instead provide intrapreneurs the tools and infrastructure to run experiments to get data that makes the value of their ideas self-evident. When decisions are made with data, the best ideas win.

Companies with a prolific track record of delivering breakthrough innovations like Google benefit from a culture of experimentation where employees are encouraged to come up with new ideas and test them. Every company, big or small, can deploy an experimentation culture by teaching intrapreneurs how to run lean experiments on their ideas

The Nice Accountant

Patty's team ran several Hack Days and Pain Jams and diligently held postpartums afterwards discussing ideas for improvement. Derwin continued to be a regular attendee.

After a Hack Day with accountant customers, Boris relayed a story:

> During the gallery walk, I happened to notice one of the accountants, Yvonne Domingo, give the budgeting app team 100 Prizmic Dollars. I followed her and asked her what she liked about the idea.
>
> She said "Budgets are very important. You'll be surprised how many of my clients don't have a budget. Then they wonder why their accounts are always a mess I have to clean up!"
>
> I thought that was a great answer. "Great, will you use it if it gets released to market?"
>
> "Oh no," she said. "An app like that would never work for me. I need budgets integrated in my accounting software."
>
> "Really? Then why did you give them the Prizmic Dollars?" I asked.
>
> "Well, they seemed like really nice guys and they had worked so hard. I had to give them *something!*"

"Arrgh!" Patty groaned. "That's not what we wanted her to do. We explained to the customers that they should only give Prizmic Dollars to products they would use themselves!"

"It doesn't surprise me Patty," Carol said. "It's human nature to want to be nice."

"Yes, but being nice in this case isn't helpful," Patty said. "It defeats the whole purpose of replacing senior leaders as judges."

"I agree," Boris said. "That's why I'm bringing it up. I'm not sure what we can do to fix it."

"Maybe we can try being clearer with customers that we don't want them to be nice," Carol offered.

"Ha ha! Yeah, we're Prizmic. We're all a bunch of jerks. Don't be nice to us!" Boris joked.

"Or maybe instead of our fake Prizmic money, we should award points to teams based on how many business cards they collect. The fact that a customer is willing to commit time to help the team with the idea is a stronger confirmation of interest," Patty suggested.

"You know this discussion makes me think of something," Derwin interjected. "Have you guys heard of the Lean Startup?"

"Is that the Eric Ries guy who has a blog? Doesn't he write about startups?" Patty asked.

"Yes, that's him. Lean Startup is his book out now and it's excellent! He talks about the folly of asking customers hypothetical questions. They might tell us they would use a product out of politeness," Derwin said.

"Are we asking our customers hypothetical questions?" asked Boris.

"Yes we are! The Prizmic dollars we're asking them to invest isn't real, so there's no real commitment to the choices they are making. That's why Yvonne invested in an idea she wouldn't use," Derwin replied.

"OK, I see what you mean. What does Eric Ries suggest we do then?" Boris asked.

"It starts with the assertion that every idea is based on things we know and things we assume. We never know if the things we assume are true until customers interact with our product. Instead of asking hypothetical questions, in the Lean Startup methodology, we develop a minimal product and offer it to customers to use 'for real' to test our assumptions.

"For example, to test the assumption that people would be willing to pay for a product, we would run an experiment where we ask them to actually buy the product and see if they bite. The difference is we're measuring actual customer behavior. He calls the data you collect from measuring customer behavior 'customer-validated learning.' We then use what we learn to improve our idea. You keep iterating on your solution until you have tested all your important assumptions."

"It does sound very similar to design thinking especially the part about iterating solutions with customers," Carol said. "In fact, the work we did with HR on New Hire Orientation employed design thinking and running experiments. So how is the Lean Startup any different?"

"The two are not mutually exclusive and as you just said, they are very similar in how they use rapid experimentation as the key to learning what solutions will work with customers. The Lean Startup really drills down into experimentation and focuses on providing startups a quantitative approach to eliminating uncertainties and steering to success.

"The 'lean' part of the Lean Startup is about reducing waste. When a startup spends a year building out a product which eventually fails in the market, that year was a huge waste. Especially if they could have learned much earlier on with quick experiments that the idea was flawed and how to fix it to make it work."

"I do like the notion of a process that keeps teams from falling so much in love with their solutions that they forget the customer," Carol said. "It's like design thinking for techies."

"Yes, I think of it as a management process for the startup team with customer-validated learning as the true measure of progress. That's better than metrics like lines of code or arbitrary milestones which don't let you know whether you're simply spinning your wheels," Derwin added.

"Derwin, that all sounds great. But how does this solve our judging problem?" Boris asked.

"Well, if instead of having a panel of judges, you could give prizes to teams that accumulated the most customer-validated learning."

"How the heck do you do that?" Boris asked.

"I don't know," Derwin answered. "But I think it's worth figuring out."

"Well this is a great discussion," Patty chimed in. "I'm going to give each of us homework. Let's all read Eric Ries' book and next week let's reconvene to see if there's anything of value to us."

Becoming a Lean Startup

At the next team meeting, Boris was particularly passionate about what he had just read. "I see now that everything we've been doing was just innovation theater!"

Patty was a little bemused. "Please say more."

"Well, we know nothing about the value of any of these projects until they get into customers' hands. Our Hack Days are a complete waste of time!"

"I wouldn't call it a complete waste of time!" Carol objected. "Look at all the energy that's generated during the Hack Days. I know several employees have said they are grateful to have a forum where they can work on their ideas with visibility from senior leaders. Also, bringing customers into Hack Days has definitely helped make the teams more customer-focused."

"OK, apart from increasing employee engagement and customer focus, it's a waste of time!" Boris insisted.

"What are you talking about?" Carol exclaimed. "Those are big deals!"

Patty was enjoying the back-and-forth but finally looked like she could wait no longer. "No, I wouldn't call it a waste of time. After all, 'Voice-It,' one of our biggest Whitespace Time success stories was birthed at a Hack Day. "I think Hack Days had a valuable role to play in helping get Whitespace

Time off the ground and they still benefit the company. But I agree we can do much better. Reading Eric Ries' book makes me think we should also be doing something other than Hack Days."

"Yes," Boris said. "We've got to make every Whitespace team that's building a customer solution a lean startup."

"Say more, what do you mean by that?" Carol asked.

"Every team should run the Build-Measure-Learn loop. It's not enough for them to just come up with ideas. We should help them build their experiments so they can measure real customer behavior and learn what's good about their ideas and what needs to be changed. Then they run the loop again and again each time improving the idea. They should only present to senior leaders when the data from their experiments shows their project is winning with customers."

"I like that idea!" Carol said. "The Lean Startup methodology could also help teams working on internal tools and process improvements. In this case, their customers are other employees."

"Boris, I like how you said we should make every Whitespace Time team building a solution for customers or making internal process improvements a lean startup. That would be a very inspiring mission for our team," Patty said.

"You know what, it's not just the Whitespace teams that should be lean startups," Carol said. "Our team should be a lean startup! We should be build-measure-learning as well!"

"We've kind of been doing that we've our Hack Day postpartums," Patty said.

"Yes, but the Lean Startup methodology will make us more rigorous at measuring and learning. It will be good to practice what we preach!" Carol asserted.

"No doubt!" Patty agreed.

"OK, this is a great discussion and I don't want to be the wet blanket," Boris said. "But helping teams with iterations of the Build-Measure-Learn loop implies we have a more long-lived engagement with each team. We're already so busy with Hack Days. When are we going to find time to do that?"

"That's a good question Boris," Patty answered. "I'll bring this up with Sebastian at our next one-on-one meeting. I'm hoping he's ready to give us more funding to expand the team."

"Awesome! We'll keep our fingers crossed!" Boris said with a smile.

Commentary: The Lean Startup

The Lean Startup Methodology is a key part of your intrapreneur's toolkit. By focusing on how to measure customer behavior, some forms of experimentation can return a measurable result, direct from customers, quickly and inexpensively. Then the team can assess whether their initial assumption of what would work, their hypothesis, was correct or not. This disciplined approach to iteratively testing to learn, and develop solutions that actually work for the customer, constitute Eric Ries' Build-Measure-Learn Feedback Loop.

The Build-Measure-Learn Feedback Loop is a process that people can apply to almost any situation where a solution is needed. All that is needed to start this "loop" is a point of view regarding what a solution might do.

The first "**build** step" means constructing a physical representation of the solution. This prototype "thing" that is built doesn't need to be complete. The minimal "build" to learn what needs to be learned is the best approach. For example, if a team is learning whether a mobile sports camera can work for surfers, they need not build a complete system including a mounting system, special camera, custom-fitting enclosure, or other details. In fact all GoPro first assembled was a small, stock wide angle camera placed into a cheap plastic enclosure which they duct-taped to the back of a surfboard. Then the "test surfers' evaluated the resulting footage. Similarly, to test a new dashboard navigation system for a line of cars, an entire new test navigation system - an estimated 16 months of work - did not need to be built. Instead, Toyota taped an iPad running a new user interface flow to the dashboard of a Camry and had test drivers use the new interface. That prototype took 2 weeks to build rather than 64 weeks.

When a prototyped solution is built, it may be given to customers in a number of different ways. An **in-market experiment** means the solution is delivered out to customers as if it were living, unconstrained and fully deployed in the marketplace. Another way to test is to only give a select number of customers the solution.

To complete the loop, one way or another, the thing that is built is presented to the customer. This thing could be a webpage, a bare bones app, a physical item, or anything at all that is functional. When the customer takes what is built, their action is measured.

Learning starts by evaluating whether the customer action was the expected one or not. Did they validate the hypothesis? Was the hypothesized behavior disproven? This review of behavior is the way we learn about the solution.

The Build-Measure-Learn Feedback Loop as a fundamentally important approach to driving innovation.

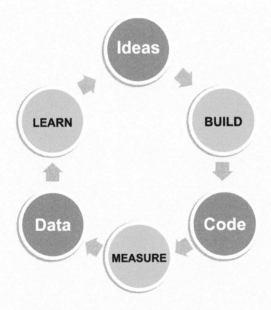

The Build-Measure-Learn Feedback Loop

The commitment to move away from opinions and to use learning coming out of the Build-Measure-Learn loop to assess progress is a huge step. When teams work this way, they're following enough of a rigorous process to validate what they learning with real, observed behavior. It is this behavior, seen in the context of answering an open "question" about a solution, that leads to customer validated learning.

The idea of "trusting the process," the iterative way of tying learning to customer behavior in relation to thoughtful experiments, changes both the pace and the object of the game. The paralysis associated with "do I have the best idea, is my idea right?" disappears. The notion of starting with the "right idea" is off the table, a non-issue. Just starting, trusting the process, and learning fast from customers becomes the healthy, unobstructed path to success.

When you convince your company to build up true capability in running experiments with customers, customer validate learning will take over as the real currency of innovative progress. And then the glossy powerpoints and opinion-laden-judges will go away.

Think of your Whitespace teams as internal lean startups. When each innovation team becomes committed to rapid experimentation with customers, then the characteristics of how teams behave will change.

And every function in the company can itself act as a lean startup, continuously improving and evolving their own processes via experimentation. This insight is an offshoot of the "dog fooding" concept. But as you inspire every team to be a lean startup, to measure progress via the Build-Measure-Learn loop, your functions, internal innovations, as well as end-user innovations, improved innovation results will quickly appear on the horizon.

Letting Go

Patty was excited about the team's Lean Startup discussion. Her small team of Boris and Carol had made a big impact, but the possibilities of nurturing dozens of lean startups would be huge for Prizmic but would require more bodies. Surely, her boss, CTO Sebastian Veksler, would support her request to grow the team.

At their one-on-one meeting, Sebastian praised Patty for the team's progress. "I like how you've evolved the Hack Days and made them more customer-focused. Just yesterday, an engineering manager in the Enterprise Division was telling me how one of his engineers was arguing with his product manager about their customers' biggest pain points. The manager was so impressed because this was a very shy engineer who used to just implement whatever requirements product management would give him. Now he's actively engaged in the product discussion. His manager says it was after participating in a Hack Day with customers that brought him out of his shell and now he's a much more valuable employee."

"Thanks Sebastian, that's wonderful feedback" Patty said. "Yes, once engineers get a taste of wearing the product management hat and working directly with customers on their Whitespace Time project, it makes them behave differently back on their day job."

"Yes, and that's a huge benefit to the organization. So what's next for your team? How do we spread more goodness throughout the company?"

"I'm glad you asked! We have a vision of making every Whitespace Time team in the company that's building solutions for customers a lean startup." Patty went on to explain that meant each team would run experiments in market and would keep iterating until they have customer success.

"That sounds fantastic! When do you start?" Sebastian asked.

"Not so fast! I also want to host more Hack Days and have them at different locations. But they are logistically more challenging to put on and my tiny team is stretched as it is. We talked in the past about at some point expanding my team. I think now is the time."

"I love your lean startup idea. I'm not so sure about creating a bigger Hack Days team though."

"But Hack Days are still important!" Patty protested.

"Don't you have Whitespace Time Champions? Why not let go of organizing Hack Days and let that community take over? Have you done enough to where you have a template that others can use?"

"I'm not sure how well that will work. Besides, we'll still need a bigger team for the lean startup vision."

"Fair enough. I suggest you start by freeing your team up from running Hack Days. Then come back with a proposal on what team you'll need for the lean startup vision."

Patty knew she was being pushed but it still took a few hours of reflection after the meeting to appreciate Sebastian's prodding. Hack Days would certainly scale more effectively across the company if her team wasn't involved in organizing every one. Furthermore, true culture change would be realized when Hack Days were occurring organically throughout the organization.

She shared these reflections later with the team. "What do you think if we delegate Hack Days to the Whitespace Time community?"

A little to her surprise, Boris and Carol were enthusiastic about the idea. "That definitely makes sense," Boris said. Boris had been responsible for organizing the Whitespace Champions and led a meeting with them every month. "In fact, some champions have already been organizing their own events."

Carol agreed. "I'm sure each champion will put her or his own spin on Hack Days. If we consider each one as an experiment and learn what works and what doesn't, we'll get much more learning than if we're organizing all the events ourselves."

"I'm glad you're both supportive," Patty said. "Freeing up our time from Hack Days will allow us to focus on how to turn our teams into lean startups."

The team wrote up "How to run an effective Hack Day" and shared it with the whole company. The idea was that anyone from a handful of employees to a whole division would now be empowered to run their own event. **[See Resource: "How to run an effective Hack Day"]**[1]

---

[1]Page 197

Commentary: Reaching Across the Enterprise

The right central resources, with the know-how to increase innovation, can be a game-changer for companies looking to up their innovation game. But the answer to scalability questions is often not "more official resources are better."
Volunteers, or "champions" run on passion and belief, and can take a company far. These champions serve as linchpins and may be the best answer to scaling things like Hack Days company-wide.

You can leverage endorsements from the top to engage leader's recruitment help across your company. And the best way to increase the crop of Whitespace Champions is to identify the most passionate representatives within each division.

When identifying champions, you must be careful. What's needed are true volunteers, not "the volunteered." If the champions aren't really passionate about Whitespace Time they can do more harm than good. So passion for Whitespace Time is the primary criteria. And the ability to drive, influence, and coach are also key factors to a champion's success.

After identifying the most passionate people as champions, the center must guide and enable. Your dedicated innovation team members are carriers of the torch. They provides the tools, mindsets and expertise that champions use.
Within each organization, the approaches may be customized. Variations can be "run as an experiment where we can learn what works and what doesn't." But the central resources own the goals, tools, and framing of the company-wide program. It is their responsibility to get great at coaching each champion. Driving a great outcome from within the organizations becomes a shared responsibility.

By establishing clear top-down support, reaching out to each division, and installing a network of champions, a company can increase the odds of driving great results from the center. If the volunteers are passionate, and the coaching is spot-on, a network of "volunteer" champions can be the most effective way to scale capability across your company.

The Champions Take Over

The following year, there were predictably successful and problematic manifestations of Hack Days as champions took over.

The Enterprise Division decided one day for a Hack Day wasn't enough time to develop working code. Also, Hack Days would be more effective if everybody participated so that participants wouldn't be pulled away by their day job. Instead, they launched every quarter three consecutive "Innovation Days."

Furthermore, Enterprise Division GM Walter Hicks wanted to direct the Whitespace Time efforts onto his high priority problems. He found a way to do it without infringing on the employees' autonomy was by issuing "Grand Challenges" to employees. One Grand Challenge was to come up with a way to reduce the deployment time for a new client by 50%. **[See Resource: Prizmic Enterprise Division's Grand Challenge]**[1]

The Enterprise Division would go on to produce the most graduates of Whitespace Time ideas to formally funded initiatives and the Enterprise Division would rank top in the company for number of employees who utilized Whitespace Time.

One experiment that failed badly came from the Consumer Division. Product Manager Heidi Brazle and Senior Architect Vikram Agrawal came up with the idea for a Consumer Division Shark Tank event. They were both big fans of the "Shark Tank" ABC TV series where budding entrepreneurs present their ideas to business titans for their considerations for investment. They imagined a four week process where teams would work on their ideas, get feedback along the way, and a winner selected at the end. In this case, the "sharks" would be the Consumer Division GM Dan Lewinsky and his staff. The winner would be guaranteed formal funding.

When Patty heard the idea, she was very concerned. "Vikram, we've learned that having senior leaders as judges is problematic. We've found the best presented ideas win, not necessarily the best ideas. You should instead

---

consider having customers pick the winner."

Vikram was unmoved. "Customers will be part of the process as the teams will be encouraged to run their ideas by them over the course of the month. Also, each team will present their customer evidence as part of their final presentation."

Patty was still concerned but didn't feel she should stand in the way. Clearly Vikram and the Consumer Division were excited about the Shark Tank event. Also, in the spirit of experimentation, it would be insightful to see how things would go.

Unfortunately, the Shark Tank event ran into numerous problems. The Consumer Division GM staff were eagerly involved in what they considered coaching the teams. However, the teams felt instead like they were being micromanaged and had lost the autonomy to direct their own projects. A couple of teams complained that their idea had been completely changed by the senior executives.

Worse still, at the end of the month, the team that had developed an event planner application was selected the winner, but contrary to what they had been promised, their project was not given formal funding. Instead, Allison Tan, the VP of Product Management for the Consumer Division announced that none of the Shark Tank projects met the strategic high bar for the division. Instead, those resources would be assigned to a new project the leadership team had identified.

Vikram, who had a history of frustration with Whitespace Time, was livid. "They reneged on a promise!" he complained later to Patty.

Patty and her team subsequently discussed the Shark Tank debacle. "So that experiment went badly. What did we learn from it? Let's start with some positives."

"I love that the Consumer Division was looking to source their new project from Whitespace Time ideas. Obviously it didn't work out but it's still a huge positive that they even considered it," Carol said.

"I guess there was a lot of positive engagement until the very end. Some teams enjoyed the attention from senior leaders," Boris added.

"Anything else," Patty asked. After a long pause she said "Negatives?"

Boris sealed his lips, looking tense. "Don't make promises you don't intend to keep."

"I think it was sad that despite their best intentions, so many senior leaders did such a shoddy job of coaching," Carol said. "Perhaps we can provide guidance on how to be an effective coach?"

"That's an excellent point Carol," Patty said. "I've had two really great coaches in my career. My former boss Rowan and my current boss Sebastian. I always felt they gave me good guidance without feeling like I couldn't make my own decisions."

"That's one good coaching attribute. There are many others. Like using inquiry before advocacy. Or not always feeling you have to have the right answer, instead ask the right question," said Carol.

Boris said, "That resonates with me. Have you heard of Bill Campbell? He's one of Silicon Valley's titans and is renowned for coaching so many successful leaders. He said you had to teach teachers how to teach. I think we need to teach leaders how to coach."

"That's great!" Carol said. "I can develop a how to be a better coach curriculum with that as a starting point." **[See Resource: <u>Coaching Tips</u>]**[1]

"We haven't yet talked about one of the biggest problems," Boris said.

"What is it?" Patty asked.

"The coaches interactions with teams is still too much about opinions. If the team has an opinion and the coach, who happens to be a senior leader, has a different opinion, whose opinion do you expect will win?"

"Probably the HIPPO's," said Patty.

---

[1] Page 261

"The hippo's?" said Carol.

"Yes, that's an acronym that stands for the Highest Paid Person's Opinion" answered Patty.

"Ha! Very clever!" Carol remarked. "So how do we get out of HIPPO decisions?"

"We need to have an experimentation culture like they have at Google," Boris said. "Instead of debating opinions, people should run experiments and let the data settle the argument."

"I agree Boris," said Patty. "But we lack so much of the infrastructure Google has that makes running experiments easy."

"Well, I'm sure Google didn't build their infrastructure in a day. We need to start."

Evolving the Team

Patty's team continued to survey the company every quarter on Whitespace Time usage which they would share in the "What's the Whitespace Time?" newsletter emailed to the entire company **[See Resource: "What's the Whitespace Time?" Newsletter]**[1] . The utilization measured consistently fell between 40% to 60% of employees. This was a far cry from the 8% measured before her team was formed. The team felt like utilization around 50% was healthy. There were always going to be employees who simply weren't interested in taking on self-directed projects. 50% felt like a level where the employees who wanted to use Whitespace Time were not being blocked from doing so. The survey indicated about 60% of employees were using the time to build new solutions for customers. The rest were evenly split between internal improvements and learning new skills. The team would continue to monitor utilization every other quarter to ensure it stayed at a healthy level, but would now focus on other opportunities.

With her team freed up from running Hack Days, Patty focused on putting together a proposal for a team to help turn Whitespace Time teams into lean

[1] Page 230

startups. She shared the challenge with her team. "What do we need to do to help teams turn their ideas into in-market experiments?"

Carol went first. "I know a common pain point I hear is teams have lack of resources. Designers are particularly hard to come by. And if the team is from HR or Legal, they have trouble finding engineers to work on their idea."

Boris joined in. "Yes, designers are hard to come by. Engineers, not so much. We try to play matchmaker to help teams that don't have engineers find engineers. If they can't get an engineer to join them, perhaps that's a reflection on their idea."

"Or perhaps an indication that we should do a better job of matchmaking," Patty said.

"A bigger problem to me is getting anything by Legal," Boris said. "Once you talk about releasing something to customers, you need legal sign-off. And that can take weeks and we've had situations where the idea died on the vine waiting for Legal."

"That's true. Remember Project Jasmine? That was the team that wanted to release an experiment of a Arabic-localized app in the Middle East? The Legal team had a huge freak out," said Patty.

"Yes, wasn't that team scolded for coming up with something so crazy?" Boris said.

"OK, clearly there are a lot of challenges. What's the best way to flesh out a list?" asked Patty.

"Well, I'm organizing an offsite of Whitespace Time champions at the end of the month. They would be the perfect group to brainstorm issues they are seeing with getting experiments into customers' hands," Boris said.

"That's a great idea!"

At the Whitespace Time Champions Offsite, Patty led a brainstorm on experimentation blockers and together they came up with a prioritized list of problems to solve:

- Coaching teams on how to turn their ideas into experiments
- Supplement teams with design and engineering help
- Make it easier for teams to get web server resources
- Speed up functional approval – Legal, Security, Privacy, and Marketing
- Provide a channel for customers to discover their experiments
- Make running experiments easy, including instrumenting applications and collecting data

Senior PM Derwin Reese, the Consumer Division Whitespace Time champion, remarked at the end: "Most important, teams want hands-on help. They get enough opinions on what they should do and not enough help making it happen."

Patty used the priorities to determine the composition of her team. She would ask to hire six engineers, two designers and a program manager.

Based on an idea she had heard from Google Labs, she also wanted to solve the problem that teams need the most focused time when they are initially get a project off the ground. The Google Labs team provided teams with a week to focus on building the initial version of their project which they would then be able to complete over time in their 20% time. Patty wanted to try something similar for Whitespace Time teams at Prizmic, helping them operate as lean startups.

The name she used for her new team in the proposal was "Prizmic Labs" which she felt reflected the team's expanded charter beyond nurturing Whitespace Time. **[See Resource: Prizmic Labs Proposal]**.[1]

Selling the New Mission

Sebastian loved Patty's proposal. He asked her to give a summary of what she was planning at his monthly meeting with the heads of engineering. Patty would have 30 minutes to provide a summary and get feedback.

Aiden Mendonca, the just hired VP of Engineering for Mobile was the first to give feedback. "At my previous startup, we employed the Lean Startup methodology. Our founder was an ex-Googler and his mantra was 'Say it with data.' The Lean Startup jibes really well with that philosophy."

George Wells, the VP of Engineering for the Consumer Division who had been promoted to take over from Rowan Sandhu, was not so convinced. "You know, I've read the Lean Startup book and it has a few good concepts but I don't know if it works for a bigger company like ours."

"But George, in the book, Eric Ries describes how Intuit, which is a pretty big company, was able to successfully use the methodology," Patty said.

"I don't know. If you start off with a bad idea, I don't care how many times you iterate, you're not going to end up with a good idea," George said. "It seems the key to me is starting off with good ideas."

"How do we know what a good idea is? Isn't that the point?" Sebastian said.

"Well I know what a good idea is!" George exclaimed.

"You do? How can you tell?" asked Aiden.

"Well from my experience. I've seen lots of ideas and know what a good idea looks like," George said.

"Wow! If you're this amazing evaluator of ideas, how come you're not making a ton of money working with a Venture Capitalist on Sand Hill Road?" asked Aiden.
Patty couldn't resist jumping in.

"Yes George, did you invest early in Google, Amazon, or Facebook? Seems like you'd be very rich by now!"

"Now, now. Let's not all jump on George's case," Sebastian interrupted. "He's expressing a doubt that lots of people will have. It does seem important to explain how we're building a culture which relies less on opinion and more on data."

"Yes, the Lean Startup doesn't eliminate the value of good judgment and experience. It just increases our odds of success and reduces the waste of building out something we could have learned early on was doomed for failure," Patty said.

There were no other objections to Patty's proposal and Sebastian gave her the go-ahead to expand her team. Finally, after almost a year, she was going to be able to add new team members!

Going Sailing

Patty received a deluge of applications after posting her job openings on Prizmic's internal job openings website. It turned out that working on a team that behaved like a startup and helped other teams work like effective startups had wide appeal. In less than six weeks, she had filled her job openings which included engineer Pankaj Aron from the original Whitespace Time Task Force. She also hired engineers Elaine Hsu, Gavin Huff, and Yuri Goldstein and designer Wendy Floyd. Her external hires were designer Kevin Leahy who had worked at a string of startups, engineers Komal Ranganathan and Samir Shenoy, and program manager Michael English.

Patty's team had grown from three members to twelve. Working with Boris and Carol had been a luxury because it was easy to stay on the same page and make course adjustments when needed. Now she needed to make sure the larger team trusted each other and were all behind the same mission. Patty decided to take her new team on a two-day offsite to work on strategy and team building.

She asked the team to suggest team building activities. She would collect suggestions and have the team vote. Patty tended not to like consensus decision making when it came to decisions at work because that usually ended up with least common denominator decisions that took a long time to resolve. But in this case, she felt it was important that everyone on the team be excited about the activity.

Kevin, the new designer, had suggested sailing as a team building event. It got the most votes from the team but a couple of people, including Patty, were apprehensive.

"I've never gone sailing in my life and I don't know how to swim!" Komal protested.

"Don't worry," Kevin reassured. "Sailing is extremely safe, we'll all have life vests, and each boat will have a captain who definitely knows what their doing. The fact that most of us haven't sailed will make this a very effective team building activity. We'll have to trust each other and a little anxiety makes for powerful learning!"

The team encamped at a hotel in Jack London Square in Oakland which was right next to the dock from where the team on the first day got to race two sailboats on the San Francisco Bay. The weather turned out to be perfect for sailing that day and every single team member had a phenomenal time and got to practice relying on each other and getting comfortable with being uncomfortable.

Defining Intrapreneurship Week

On the second day, the team got down to business with a working session in one of the hotel's conference rooms. Patty had thought long about how she would open with the team. "Prizmic is committed to innovation and is making the investments we need to stay a vibrant and growing company for years to come. The fact that all of us are here now is a testament to Prizmic's commitment. Our challenge is to make sure these investments pay off. We don't want to be mere producers of innovation theater. Hack Days have been a good start but now it's time to start putting points on the board."

Boris interrupted. "How do you suggest we put points on the board? That sounds like we'd have to sign up for business metrics which in my opinion is a losing proposition. Historically, it's taken at least five years for successful new products at Prizmic to gain meaningful revenue. But we're measured on performance every year so anything we do in a particular year will look meaningless to the rest of the company."

"Yes, Boris, that is a challenge every company that invests in the long term must deal with. How do you gauge how well those investments are doing in the short term?" Patty said. "A lot has been written on the subject of 'Innovation Accounting.' I don't think there's a perfect answer but Eric Ries' book gives us an important clue. Does anyone remember what Eric says is the unit of progress for lean startups?"

"Customer-validated learning!" answered Carol and Pankaj almost simultaneously.

"That's right. It's not the number of lines of code. It's not how many features have been completed. If we're going to turn Whitespace Time Teams into lean startups, we must fully embrace customer-validated learning as our performance measure."

"That sounds good. But how do we measure customer-validated learning? Will our metrics even make sense to the rest of the company?" Boris asked.

"Let's be very clear. A big part of our jobs will be education. We'll have to be both practitioners and teachers of the Lean Startup Methodology. This includes being very adept at explaining our metrics and how they tie to long-term revenue growth, which is our ultimate goal."

Patty paused to let that sink in. "For Prizmic, I think we can start with a very basic measure. So much of the work Whitespace Time Teams have done never leaves the Prizmic campus. We need to change the culture so that teams are hungry to put their products into customers' hands instead of just impressing executives with a flashy demo. I propose we measure number of experiments."

"And by experiments, you mean in-market experiments?" Carol asked.

"Yes, thanks for the clarification Carol. We're counting experiments where we collect customer-validated learning."

"To collect customer-validated learning, each team will need to produce a Minimum Viable Product," Pankaj added.

"That's right Pankaj!" Patty said. "Please remind everybody what is a Minimum Viable Product, or MVP in Lean Startup parlance."

"Well that's the product you deliver to customers that has only the features you need to gather your customer-validated learning," he said.

"Thank you Pankaj. As our signature offering to the organization, I would like to propose every month we hold an 'Intrapreneurship Week.' We will host Whitespace Time teams during that week who would come to us on Monday with an idea and by Friday would have an MVP ready to release to customers."

"Releasing a product to customers in just one week? Is that even possible?" new team member Gavin asked.

"Remember it's an MVP," Patty said.

"Yes, but what about all the bureaucratic process in getting a product ready for customers? We'll need all kinds of signoff. Marketing, Data Hosting, Privacy, and oh my God, Legal!" Gavin pushed back. "In my experience, any request to our legal department alone takes at least one week to get resolved!"

"You're right. Those are exactly the kinds of challenges our team needs to streamline so that Whitespace Teams are no longer stymied by them," Patty said.

"I hate to be the party-pooper but I just don't think one week is possible. Not here at Prizmic," Gavin said.

"I don't know Gavin, I think we won't know unless we try," said Pankaj.

"It sounds like we have a leap-of-faith assumption," said Boris.

"Say more Boris," Patty asked with a slight smile. "And remind everyone what a leap-of-faith assumption is."

"Leap-of-faith assumptions are the assumptions we make about an idea which if they don't out to be true, the whole idea falls apart. We've talked about how our own team should operate as a lean startup. If you think about it, Intrapreneurship Week itself is our product and we're assuming that teams can create MVPs in one week. Instead of having this debate, let's test and learn!"

"Thank you Boris!" Patty said. "You're right, we should not only talk to teams about being lean startups but we should practice what we preach. Also, as an innovation team, we have to live the ethos of fearless innovators. That anything is possible. If we are too afraid to take something on, what does that say for the rest of the company?"

"Anything is possible?" Gavin repeated with an eye roll.

"Yes! The most important innovations in history all seemed impossible until someone took them on. Whether it was the Wright Brothers being first to flight or Google creating an index of the entire Internet!" Patty said.

Elaine, who had been fairly quiet finally jumped in. "I think Mohammed Ali once said 'Impossible is not a fact. It's an opinion.'"

"Fine, but will employees be able to sign up for a whole week? Will their managers let them?" Gavin asked.

"Well they have their 10% Whitespace Time. If they haven't used it in three months, they would have banked enough. It shouldn't be any different than scheduling vacation," Pankaj explained.

"That's only if the managers are supportive of Whitespace Time," Gavin said.

"Sounds like we have another leap-of-faith assumption. Can we get ten teams to sign up for Intrapreneurship Week?" Boris interjected.

Patty was pleased in spite of Gavin's doubts, the rest of team seemed to be with her. "From now on, we take on the impossible!"

Boris got the last word in: "Speaking of impossible, who's going to take on Legal?"

Conclusion

Unenlightened managers believe their role is to serve as arbiters of good ideas. But successful innovation companies instead learn from customers. Great leaders, the kind that enable and inspire intrapreneurs, recognize that their opinions are likely to undervalue the most disruptive ideas. These great leaders instead provide intrapreneurs the tools and infrastructure to run experiments to get customer learning data that makes the value of their ideas self-evident. When decisions are made with this data, the best ideas win.

Companies with a prolific track record of delivering breakthrough innovations like Google benefit from a culture of experimentation where employees are encouraged to come up with new ideas and test them. Every company, big or small, can deploy an experimentation culture by teaching intrapreneurs how to quickly run inexpensive, effective experiments.

CHAPTER 7
ALIGN FOR YES

"The first responsibility of a leader is to define reality.
The last is to say thank you.
In between, the leader is a servant."
- Max de Pree

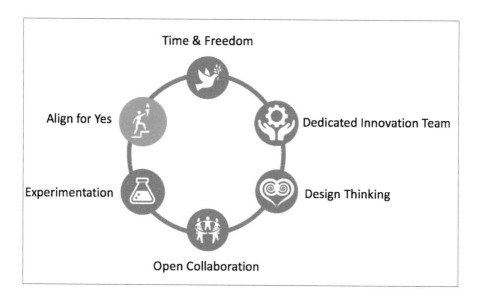

Introduction

Unhelpful managers allocate all their resources to top-down initiatives, within silos, during budget planning. They are either disinterested observers or unhelpful meddlers as intrapreneurs attempt to make progress. But great leaders operate differently. They set aside resources so that future promising employee-driven initiatives can be adequately supported. They provide alignment and connection across the company so that boundaries disappear, silos dissipate, and the company mission may be realized.

In this way great leaders connect, unblock, and foster the kind of strategic vision that serves to open gateways for intrapreneurs.

When multiple organizations are connect, aligned, and are working in service of the big picture view of customer benefit, everyone is more amenable to supporting customer innovation. Working together towards the common, fully aligned strategy helps teams - even teams from disparate functions across the company -- find a way to collaborate, moving past the bureaucratic stock answer of "no", and instead "getting to yes".

Partnering

Despite Patty's bold proclamations at the offsite, she harbored her own trepidation about how to come up with a streamlined approach to get legal approval for Whitespace Time MVPs. In her long tenure at Prizmic, she hadn't always had the best experience with the legal department. She remembered how she felt early in her tenure when a lawyer sent her an email and copied everyone in her group where he rebuked her for using unlicensed images on the product website.

Then there was Project Jasmine, a Whitespace Time team that was never able to get a go-ahead from Legal. That experience hurt because that team consisted of three recent college hires whose excitement over their idea turned into disengagement when they weren't able to move forward after a terse "cease-and-desist" message from one of the legal counsels.

She went to Sebastian to get his advice on how to move forward. Sebastian was very optimistic about move forward. "I have a great relationship with our General Counsel Olivia and she's very supportive of innovation. Let's schedule a meeting for the three us to discuss how to move forward."

A week later when they met with Olivia, Patty was pleasantly surprised to find she was a sympathetic audience as she described Intrapreneurship Week and her goals for streamlining legal approval.

"You know, Legal gets a bad rap for getting in the way of progress. Of course we have to watch out for the company and ensure we don't take on imprudent legal exposure. But our main goal is to partner with other functions to find solutions so instead of just saying 'no,' we can help find a way to 'yes'," said Olivia.

"That sounds wonderful but it doesn't always work that way," replied Patty who went on to describe the Project Jasmine debacle.

"I suppose some of our lawyers may forget this partnership mindset. This is the first time I'm hearing about Project Jasmine. In the future, I'd like you to escalate directly to me any time Legal has become a hurdle," Olivia said.

"I would love to have you work with us on Intrapreneurship Week. I'm sure we can find a reasonable way forward. Plus our partnership will be a teachable moment for the organization when they see my team working effectively with the innovation team. Give me a couple of days to assign someone to work with you."

Patty left the meeting with Olivia reflecting on two important insights. First, she must work across functional lines to develop relationships like the one Sebastian had with Olivia. Removing organizational barriers is so much easier when you're working with a friend. Second, she had to be less bashful about escalation. She couldn't help wondering if she shared the blame for Project Jasmine's demise by not raising the flag.

Working with Legal

The next week, Patty and Boris met with Deputy Counsel Humberto Rodriguez and Paralegal Christine Chen. Humberto and Christine had been well prepped by Olivia for the meeting and came already equipped with ideas on how to streamline approval.

"You know there not that many things that can get you into real trouble with a new product," Humberto explained. "For example, with the name of the product, we don't want to infringe on another company's trademark rights. Teams get into trouble when they try to come up with cutesy names. If they just keep the name functional, like 'Prizmic Budgets', they are much less likely to run into problems."

"That's right," Christine added. "We can provide naming guidelines."

"That's wonderful," Patty said. "What other guidelines can your provide? If teams abide by your checklist, will that help us meet our goal of releasing to customers in a week?"

"I don't see why we can't make that happen," Humberto replied. "We'll just need someone from our department to review what they've done."

"Oh oh. I don't like the sounds of that. How long will that take? Sometimes you guys get busy and it's hard to schedule time," said Patty.

"Oh don't worry about that. Just let us know when and where you'll be holding your Intrapreneurship Week events. We'll be happy to come by and talk to the teams," Christine said.

"Oh wow! That sounds like great personalized service!" Patty exclaimed.

"That's why we're here, to be your partners in Intrapreneurship Week," said Humberto with a smile.

A week later, Christine sent Patty a legal checklist which the team posted on their internal website. **[See Key Resource: "Legal Checklist"]**[1]. The partnership with Legal was working so well, Patty realized she had a template on how to collaborate with other functions.

Working with IT

The next challenge on Patty's list was to streamline provisioning of server resources for Whitespace Time teams. Many teams had complained how difficult it was to get server resources so that external customers could access the products they had developed. The common refrain was: "If we were working in a startup, it would take us 10 minutes to set up a server using Amazon's Web Services." In fact, several rogue teams had used corporate purchase cards to do just that, much to the chagrin of CIO Randy Mercer who wrote a long missive he emailed company-wide to admonish the practice. "People going off the reservation are making the company vulnerable to major security risks," he wrote.

In fact, it was the Security team that posed the biggest hurdle to making it easy for employees to get access to server resources. Patty again reached out to Sebastian who again facilitated a meeting with Randy. Randy was not as easy an audience as the Chief Legal Counsel had been.

"Both of you don't understand. Security has become a huge issue for Prizmic. Companies like ours are a huge target for hackers," Randy said.

Patty didn't get flustered. She had a rehearsed response for Randy. "We agree security is a huge issue and we don't want to expose the company to more

---

[1] Page 268

risks. However, we don't want to tell teams they have to wait six weeks for web resources for a product they took one week to develop. We'd like to partner with you to find a solution that is both secure and fast to deploy."

Sebastian cocked his head and took a sharp breath. "By the way, it's not just the Whitespace Time teams that are being slowed down by our slow provisioning. Even our regular product teams have complained about how long it takes to get anything new off the ground."

"I guess if we create a standard server environment which has all our monitors and locks down the ports, that would be pretty safe. But if teams have any special requests, they are going to have to wait," Randy said.

"I'm pretty sure we can make that work," said Patty.

"Great! Let me connect you with a couple of my managers to get this going."

Working with Marketing

As word started to go around Prizmic about the upcoming Intrapreneurship Week, sometimes people would approach Patty with questions or concerns. One person was Director of Marketing Andrea Lips. She had a story to share about one of the past Whitespace Time teams.

"Four months ago, a Whitespace team launched Prizmic Shipping on our main product page. Now first of all, the product did almost nothing that it claimed it did. I think they said that's because it was an MVP."

"That sounds right," Patty said.

"It does? Oh my! Well over eight hundred customers signed up for the product. We were then deluged with complaints on our customer forum about how the product was complete crap. When I asked the team when they were going to address these customer issues, you won't believe what they told me!"

"What did they say?"

"They said they had pivoted - whatever that means, and had stopped work on the product! We were totally left holding the bag!"

Patty explained to Andrea that "pivoting" was Lean Startup parlance for when a team decides to stop working on an idea to instead work on another idea based on what they've learned from customers using their product. "I'm sorry the Prizmic Shipping team caused you so many problems. I can see we'll need to work on giving better guidance to teams running experiments."

"I'm so happy to hear you say that," Andrea said. "If we create many more products like Prizmic Shipping, it's going to have an adverse impact of our brand. Right now, our brand stands for simplicity and quality. That's what customers expect from a Prizmic offering. When they don't experience simplicity and quality, that dilutes a brand we've spent years building up."

"You're right. We don't want to dilute the brand but we don't want to put a halt to experiments. Do you have any suggestions on how we can make that happen?" In Patty's partnership template, she would try to cast the problem as a shared one that they would solve together.

"Well, I don't think we should be using the Prizmic brand. That totally sets the wrong expectations for customers which we shouldn't be doing," Andrea said.

"What brand should we use?" Patty asked.

"How about a sub-brand like 'Prizmic Labs'? That would signal to customers that the product is not as evolved as our typical offerings. A customer who doesn't like to be the early adopter would know not to try it."

"I like 'Prizmic Labs'. That just happens to be the name of our team," Patty said.

"The sub-brand would also signal to our stakeholders that Prizmic is working on cutting edge products and technology."

"That sounds like a win-win! Should we provide other guidelines for teams?"

"Well if something is an experiment, it probably shouldn't be launched on our main product page where tens of thousands of customers will see it. We should think of finding other channels where customers can find these products."

"That sounds reasonable. I'm guessing the Prizmic Shipping team didn't need nine hundred customers to try their product to gather the data they needed to know they should pivot," Patty said. "We can also set up a Prizmic Labs website for customers to browse for our experiments."

"Oh absolutely! That would limit the number of customers we'd have to deal with when we shut down the experiment!"

Patty and her team worked with Andrea's team to develop brand guidelines for Prizmic experiments. **[See Resource "Protecting our brand with "Prizmic Labs"]**[1]. The Prizmic Labs sub-brand wouldn't just be used for just Whitespace Time projects, but any new product at Prizmic.

Conclusion

When leaders give employees the resources, tools, and mentoring to develop their self-directed projects, innovation can thrive. Leaders need to supply the necessities for intrapreneurship, and some of the necessities must come tops down. A formal process must be put in place allowing projects to "graduate" to officially funded initiatives. Leaders must also make sure that each functional unit and business unit understands the common innovation goals, seeing the goals through a customer-back lens. This level of alignment enables the cross-functional behaviors that truly support innovators.

If leadership support fails to align groups and assist the teams that need and deserve the help, promising innovations will "die on the vine." But when leadership support is in place, a multitude of innovations can move forward todramatically improve business results for the company

---

[1] Page 271

CHAPTER 8
THE CULMINATION: INTRAPRENEURSHIP WEEK

The First Intrapreneurship Week

In January 2010, the Prizmic Labs team hosted its first Intrapreneurship Week in a large conference room at the company's Menlo Park headquarters. Ten teams signed up for the challenge of building an MVP in one week. Each team was assigned their own table. To make the one week deadline real, a gallery walk open to all employees would be held on Friday afternoon to showcase the products built that week. The gallery walk would also be a way to advertise Intrapreneurship Week to employees. **[See Key Resource: Intrapreneurship Week]**[1]

Every participant was expected to clear their calendars for the week so that they could focus exclusively on building their MVP. The teams would be provided with breakfast, lunch, and dinner, and snacks to help them keep working.

The gregarious Boris served as the primary docent for the week but had insisted that Patty kick off the event. Patty didn't want to use up too much time with a long presentation but she thought it would be helpful getting clarity on what exactly a Minimum Viable Product was.

"For those of you who have read The Lean Startup, you know the definition of Minimum Viable Product is that version of a new product which allows a team to collect the maximum amount of validated learning about customers with the least effort.

"MVPs are the test vehicle we use to run experiments so we can gather customer-validated learning. We use them to test our leap-of-faith assumptions which are those critical assumptions in our idea that if they turn out to be wrong, we know the idea won't work. MVPs can take many forms but they cannot be a survey or a customer interview. Can someone tell me why?"

One participant, Peter Tembo, raised his hand. "Because a survey or an interview is not a product?"

---

[1] Page 233

"That's certainly true," Patty said. "But there's an even more fundamental reason."

Another participant, Wolf Baird spoke up. "Because we want to observe real customer behavior."

"That's right! We're not saying surveys or interviews are bad, but they don't afford us the opportunity to observe real behavior. When you ask a customer whether they will do something, they often will give a misleading answer, not for malicious reasons. We all often do things that are very different than what we'll say we do. A customer might tell you they'll buy your product out of politeness. But after you build your product, they don't end up buying it. Lean Startup avoids that quandary because every experiment involves decisions that are real to the customer."

"It's just like every year I tell my wife I'm going to lose weight!" Boris interjected drawing lots of laughs from the room.

"Yes Boris. Have you ever used that bicycle she bought you? You probably told her you would use a bike to lose weight if you had one but your behavior turned out to be very different," Patty said, appreciating the example. "So the first rule of MVPs – you will be creating real experiences for your customer. At least your customer should believe the experience to be real for the duration of the experiment."

"Is that why a web landing page counts as an MVP?" asked Peter.

"Absolutely! When a customer clicks on a landing page you've created, they believe they are purchasing or signing up for your product even if the rest of your product hasn't been built yet.

"The second rule of MVPs – only build what's necessary. Each team will start with a hypothesis they are testing and design an MVP that has only the features needed to test that hypothesis. Expect a lot of coaching from us this week because we all typically want to build too much into our MVPs. We'll be constantly challenging you on every feature you propose building to ask you why you need it.

"For certain table-stake features, like a login system, we'll help you use ready-to-use components so that you can spend most of your time on the functionality that supports testing your hypothesis.

"The third rule of MVPs – you must be able to measure your customer behavior. We are running experiments after all. You can't just throw your MVP over the wall to customers and wait by the phone. You need to instrument your MVP so you can see exactly what your customers are doing. Our team has assembled libraries so you can drop in analytics into your web or mobile apps. We will help you instrument your MVPs. Before you release to customers, we'll ask you for a documented learning plan which states what data you plan to collect to validate your hypotheses."

Peter raised his hand. "So what happens if we give our MVP to customers and the experiment fails?"

"That's a good question Peter," Patty replied. "The most important consideration is what have you learned. Sometimes when you run an experiment, you learn there were problems in the experiment design. For example, your product might have instructions that were so confusing that customers didn't understand what to do preventing you from measuring the behavior you wanted to test. In that case, you want to fix those problems and run the experiment again.

"However, if we've learned that a leap-of-faith assumption is wrong, we need to do something called a 'pivot.' A pivot is when we abandon our idea and switch to another idea that will achieve the same vision for the product. For example, if my vision is to get customers to put money into their savings accounts, one idea might be to build a mobile app to remind them. If that doesn't work, I could try a service where a live human calls them. Different ideas, same goal."

"And if the leap-of-faith assumption is right?" Peter asked.

"Ah, that's the happy path! Then we test the next leap-of-faith assumption on our list," Patty said. "That's called 'persevering' in the Lean Startup."

The Free Food App

Lean Startup Worksheet

Product Name: *Free Food App*

1. Vision - *how will your product improve customers lives?*	2. Product Idea - *how will you accomplish your vision?*
Reduce wasted food	

3. Assumptions

#	Assumption - *what do you believe that must be true for your idea to succeed?*	Leap of faith
1.	*Employees are interested in eating leftovers*	
2.	*Meeting organizers want to let people know about leftovers*	
3.	*People will download app*	*X*

Check as "Leap of faith" (LOFA) your riskiest assumptios
1. The most important to be true
2. The least proven to be true

3. Experiments

LOFA #	Hypothesis - *Declare expected outcome:* [Specific Repeatable Action] will [Expected Measurable Action Outcome]	Minimum **Viable Product** - *describe the experiment vehicle you'll use to test your hypothesis*	Results - *what data did you collect?*	Learning - *validated or invalidated? Surprises?*
3	*If we send 100 people email with link, 20 will download the app in 1 day*	*Email with link to landing page. How many click Download?*		

Each team was given a **[See Key Resource: Lean Startup Worksheet]**[1] to fill in. On the rest of the first day, Patty and her team spent most of time helping teams articulate their leap-of-faith assumptions and hypotheses they wanted to test.

One team that consisted of Clare Flores, a marketing manager, and Michael English, an engineer, had an idea they were very passionate about but needed help. "Our idea is targeted at Prizmic employees," Clare explained to Boris who was coaching them. "Whenever there are lunch meetings where food is catered, there's always tons left over. We found out that it all gets thrown away which is a tragic waste. The food can't even be donated to a food bank or shelter because it's been already served."

"I agree that's a tragedy to waste food when so many people are going

hungry," Boris said. "How do you intend to solve the problem?"
"We want to build a mobile app that tells Prizmic employees where free food is," Michael replied. "So if your meeting has ended and there's leftover food, you can take a picture which is sent out with the meeting room location as an alert to everyone with the app."

"Ah, so employees who are too cheap to buy their own lunch would just wait for these alerts?" Boris asked.

"Yes, but the bigger point is that food won't go to waste," Clare said.

"OK, that sounds like a cool idea. How can I help?" Boris asked.

"We're not sure how to fill in this worksheet," Clare said.

"No problem. Let's do it together," Boris said. "OK, the first box here says 'Vision - How will your product improve customers' lives.'"

"Yes, we got stuck on the very first one!" Clare said.

"Well let's think about your idea. What do you hope to achieve if it's successful?"

"We want to reduce wasted food," Michael replied.

"Perfect! Let's write that down!" Boris said.

"But is that improving customers' lives?" Clare asked.

"Sure it is. Certainly for anyone like you who is concerned about food waste, they will appreciate this app. Also, I like that your vision allows for you to come up with many other ideas if the app doesn't take off."

"Cool! The next field is 'Product Idea'," Michael said. "That seems straightforward. That's just the idea we described to you."

"Exactly!" Boris said.

"OK, but we also got stuck on 'Assumptions'. We're not sure what would go there," Michael said.

"An assumption is anything we don't know with certainty. A mistake innovators often make with our ideas is that we conflate what we know with what we're assuming. The Lean Startup methodology helps us tease these things apart," Boris explained. "So let's think about what assumptions you're making with your idea."

"Well we know that there's lots of leftover food from meetings. I guess we're assuming enough employees will be interested in eating it," Clare started.

"Are you kidding me? Engineers love free food!" Michael exclaimed. "The problem is there's no way to know which conference rooms on the campus have food available. And even when they see food outside a conference room, they're not sure whether it's kosher to grab it."

"Let's put it down as an assumption anyway since the app is describing a new type of behavior," Boris suggested.

"Well in that case, I guess we're assuming meeting organizers will want to let people know there's food available," Michael added.

"Yes indeed. Let's add that as another assumption. Tell me, how will people discover and download your app?" Boris asked.

"Oh, we hadn't really thought about that," Clare said. "I guess we could send out a mass email to everyone in the company with a download link."

"How many people do you think will open that email and click on the link?" Boris asked.

"That's a good question. That's exactly the kind of email I tend to ignore," Clare answered.

"Oh no, I would totally download the app. I love trying new apps," said Michael.

"It sounds like we have another assumption," said Boris. "In fact, this one seems like a good candidate for a leap-of-faith assumption because your idea won't work if you don't get enough people to download your app."

"I agree. I also feel less sure about people downloading than I do about people wanting free food and meeting organizers wanting to let people know there's food available," Michael added.

"Great! Let's look at the 'Experiments' table. It asks you to list hypotheses," said Boris.

"What's the difference between an assumption and a hypothesis?" Clare asked.

"A hypothesis is an 'if-then' statement we'll use to help us design tests for our assumption," Boris replied. "For the download assumption, we could say 'if we send X number of people an email with a link to the app, Y number of them will download it within Z number of days. Notice that the hypothesis has to be specific in action and timeframe with a measurable outcome."

"That all makes sense. But how do we determine the the X, Y, and Z?" Michael asked.

"That's a really good question. It turns out you have to use your judgment here. What numbers would you need for your idea to work?"

"Oh I see. We need to think about what would constitute enough critical mass so that the app is useful," Clare reflected. "But isn't that going to be very subjective? I might come up with a small rate and Michael might have a much higher rate."

"Yes, it will be subjective but as a rule of thumb, I suggest that you think of numbers that would convince someone who was skeptical of your idea," Boris replied. "It also helps to compare with existing apps that are distributed the same way."

"OK, maybe something like if we send 100 people the email, 20 of them will download the app in 1 day?" Clare said.

"That's very good and both of you can discuss the numbers some more. Now let's talk about the MVP. How will you test this hypothesis?" Boris asked.

"Do we even need to build the app?" Michael said.

"Excellent realization! Not at all. In fact, for this experiment, you just need to craft the email with a link to a landing page which can tell your customers this was just a test. But you'll have a measurable outcome."

After Boris' coaching, Clare and Michael were able to work on filling out the rest of their worksheet.

Building MVPs in One Week

As Patty predicted, many teams needed to be persuaded to reduce the scope of their MVPs. Participant Shara Gates was tough to convince. "If we don't implement share on Facebook, our customers will think our MVP is lame," she complained.

Carol tried to convince her. "If you ship your MVP without the Facebook Share, and customers complain that it's missing, then you'll know it's important and implement in your next release. But if they don't ask about it, maybe it's not important. They might complain about something entirely different."

Because Patty and her team were taking on the role of coaches and left decisions to each team, they could only try to persuade. For most teams, they were very influential, but in the case of Shara's team, they couldn't talk her out of implementing her Facebook Share feature.

Patty's designers Carol and Kevin and engineers Pankaj, Elaine, Gavin and Yuri rotated amongst the teams helping them with their tasks. One of the teams showed up without any engineers so they relied entirely on the help to get their MVP built.

Another service Patty's team provided to the participants was connecting them with experts. A lot of time expended in developing a new offering is a team just trying to figure out how to interface with components they've never used before. A lot of time can be saved when an expert can be found to spend time with an Intrapreneurship Week team. One of the teams was developing an app that took credit card payments. Boris had found an engineer who had led the team that built payments into Prizmic's CRM application. He was invited to spend a couple of hours with the team and was thanked with a free lunch.

By the end of the week, nine of the ten teams were able to complete their MVPs although for many of the teams, they were still making changes minutes before the gallery walk started. For Shara's team, they were still working to complete the Facebook Share feature because working with the Facebook Application Program Interfaces was proving to be a more difficult than they anticipated. They team was despondent thinking they would have to skip the gallery walk.

Gavin walked over to the team's table. "Why the long faces guys?"

"Ugh, we won't be able to finish the MVP today?" Shara said. "It's taken us too much time to figure out the Facebook APIs."

"Why don't you just take out that feature?" Gavin asked.

"Oh, not again! We already explained to Carol that it's the heart of our MVP. It doesn't make sense without it."

"Do you know that or is that an assumption?" Gavin said.

"There are enough analogous products that have the same capability, so I'd say it's something we know," Shara said.

"Well, maybe you can test that anyway and not have your MVP look lame," said Gavin.

"How would we do that?"

"Just leave in the 'Facebook Share' button, but when someone clicks on it, your app can say something like 'Coming Soon.' Then you can measure how many people click on that button."

"That's cool! That will be less than ten lines of code," said Jose Zaragoza, one of the engineers on the team.

"I guess that wouldn't be so bad. At least the MVP wouldn't look so lame," Shara said

"Let's do it!" Jose said. The team quickly got to action, happy to make the Gallery Walk.

Patty who observed most of the interaction was beaming with pride to see Gavin, who had initially been a naysayer, do such an effective job of influencing.

Each team was asked to practice their pitch on what problem their product was solving and what they were going to learn in their experiment.

The gallery walk was well attended by employees who were invited via a site-wide email. It helped that beverages and hors d'oeuvres were served. CEO Noel Spence and CTO Sebastian Veksler made time to visit the gallery walk. The teams seemed to enjoy the attention as they demoed their products to dozens of employees and answered their questions.

The Reflection

The following Monday, the Prizmic Labs team met to discuss how things went. They made good on their commitment to treat themselves as a lean startup with Intrapreneurship Week as their new solution for customers, who in this case were Prizmic employees. The Lean Startup language permeated their discussion.

Boris started. "Well I think we can put a checkmark next to our two leap-of-faith assumptions. Our first hypothesis was that if we held the Intrapreneurship Week, we would get ten teams to sign up, which happened. Our second hypothesis was that at least half the teams would complete their MVPs by the end of the week, and they all did!"

"Yes, that is good news! Anything else?" Patty asked?

The team proceeded to fill a whiteboard with "pluses" and "deltas" to capture mostly logistically what had gone well and what should be improved. For example, people liked the food but thought dinner being served at 4 pm was too early. The team felt that the Intrapreneurship Week participants could have been better prepared when they showed up on Monday. They also felt that teams without engineers shouldn't be accepted to future Intrapreneurship Weeks because they use up a lot of the Prizmic Labs team's bandwidth and it's not clear how they will be able to continue their experiments going forward.

The team also had feedback from participants to review. Participants were asked a "Net Promoter" question – "How likely are you to recommend Intrapreneurship Week to another employee at Prizmic on a scale of 0 to 10?" Every participant rated Intrapreneurship Week a 9 or a 10 indicating they were happy promoters. In their written feedback, the most cited designers Carol and Kevin as being most helpful. They especially liked that Kevin was able to create stunning visual prototypes in two hours or less. They were used to having to wait much longer when working with designers in their day jobs.

As a process, the team agreed to prioritize three items from the whiteboard to improve for the next Intrapreneurship Week. Each Intrapreneurship Week would represent an iteration of the Build-Measure-Learn loop for the Prizmic Labs team.

Not just for Whitespace Teams

The team held ten more Intrapreneurship Weeks that year (they skipped

December because of the holidays). The team became increasingly better at running the event. The Net Promoter ratings for the event stayed high. Almost every month, one or more participants remarked that this was the most fun that they had working. Also, almost every team each week completed their MVPs and the Prizmic Labs website was starting to fill up with lots of products. The vision of lean startups across Prizmic had come to fruition.

There was one unexpected surprise. An increasing number of teams that signed up for Intrapreneurship Week were formally funded teams. They had found out how effective it was to work in this way and chose to use this time to tackle a big challenge they could work on together.

The following year, the team experimented with inviting external companies to Intrapreneurship Week. The first was a small startup Summit Software who built solutions for not-for-profit firms. They wanted to integrate their donor management application with Prizmic's CRM application. Having a team from Summit sit with the CRM team was thought to be a more effective way to collaborate than having the teams meet several times over the course of what could be months before they had something working.

Having demonstrated how well Intrapreneurship Week worked with external companies, Patty wanted to use it as a way to vet potential partnerships or acquisitions. In the past, Prizmic had invested time and money in many such ventures which hadn't panned out for the business. The Makeni acquisition was by now viewed as a failure given the product failed to live up to the multi-year projections used during negotiations. Instead, Patty thought Prizmic and a potential partner could use Intrapreneurship Week to quickly build an MVP that could be tested in market so that projections could be based on real data.

Intrapreneurship Week offered lots of potential to the future of work and how teams could collaborate and test new ideas more efficiently.

During a particularly hectic gallery walk after an Intrapreneurship Week that included six Whitespace teams, two regular teams, and two external teams from a startup and a non-profit organization, Patty allowed herself a moment of reflection. She looked out the large conference room window, her eyes defocusing as her mind meandered. Was this all working as well as it seemed? A small smile crossed her face, and she shifted her weight from one foot to the other. The day she first assembled the task force seemed both like ages ago and two minutes ago. And here they were now. A *worthy journey, nice progress,* she thought. And her smile broadened.

Conclusion

Intrapreneurship Week is important for driving increased innovation for a number of reasons. The week itself is tangible and focused. Attendees know what the goal is (ship the MVP!) and when the results are due. Equally important, the attendees have coaching all week, at their fingertips. Rather than carrying around the cognitive load of 'do I need help, am I doing OK, should I seek help or ask questions?' the help is right there, built in. Your innovation enablement team will be visible, available, hands-on. That level of access provides a huge benefit.

First and foremost, whether positioned this way or not, Intrapreneurship Week is about education. For many attendees, this will be the first time they've built a real experiment. It may be the first time they've authored a learning plan or written a behavioral hypothesis.

And hearing a customer's words is one thing. But observing customer behavior in the context of the hypothesis and experiment you built, is a whole other thing.

You're likely to have Intrapreneurship Weeks obtain a high Net Promoter Score, attract funded as well as Whitespace Time teams, and - through positive word of mouth - gain the attention of organizations outside your own walls.

Intrapreneurship Weeks serve as one good example of how to bring all six facets of the Intrapreneurship model together. Attending employees are -

1. Putting their time & freedom to use on innovations they are passionate about,
2. Are part of a set of programs nurtured by a dedicated innovation team,
3. Are using Design Thinking to understand customers and develop solutions,

4. Openly collaborate with others inside (and even outside) company,
5. Run lean experiments to make swift progress on their ideas, and
6. Are Aligned for Yes as functions like legal, operations, and finance participate to enable the intrapreneurs' progress.

CHAPTER 9
EPILOGUE - SUSTAINING SUCCESS

The Paradox of Success

After investing passion and time developing an innovation program at your company, you now have a vibrant culture of innovation. Employees are empowered to work on their ideas. Employees are using design thinking and Lean Startup techniques to develop these ideas and test them with real customers. Employees are openly collaborating with each other and with customers, vendors, and partners. You've taken the Intrapreneurship Empowerment Model Assessment and your innovation program scores as "We rock!" because you're delivering on all facets of the model, with a regular pipeline of employee ideas that become new products delivering growth.

Your reward is your company now has an innovation engine and has gone from not having enough good ideas to where they will soon have too many good ideas. Ideas that are not viable are naturally being filtered out by experiments while they are in the H4 and H3 stages. When ideas are curtailed at these stages, there is little pain. The teams involved are bought into the decision to curtail because they are the ones recommending the decision. They see the data they've collected from experiments and know first hand that the idea is not tenable. Also, there are very few customers involved and not much time elapsed for them to be attached to the product.

But a few products will make it to the H2 stage, gaining good customer traction, and yet still end up being curtailed.

Why Products With Traction Die

To explain why sometimes H2 products with traction get shut down, let's take a look at a model that illustrates how a typical company selects ideas to fund.

First, a typical company has a mission statement which describes why they exist. A mission statement is a statement of purpose that goes beyond the profit motive. For example, Intuit's mission is "improving people's financial lives so profoundly they can't imagine going back to the old way." The mission statement sets the parameters of the types of markets and products the company will pursue. Intuit sells small business and tax software.

You wouldn't expect Intuit to sell groceries or create media for entertainment.

Second, companies typically have strategies which articulate how the company is going to achieve its growth goals and succeed in the marketplace. If a company is in multiple businesses, each business will typically have it's own strategy although there may be an overall company strategy that aims to create synergies between the different businesses. For example, one of Intuit's growth strategies for its QuickBooks small business accounting franchise is to enter new global markets outside North America.

Finally, companies typically have a short-term strategic focus which defines which aspects of the strategic plan are being executed in the next one to three years. For a company executing a global expansion, the strategic focus would specify which set of countries to start with.

Figure 1 is an in-focus graph with four concentric circles which illustrates how new ideas can be evaluated against a company's mission, strategy, and focus. Ideas that align with all three fall in the center of the graph. These are the ideas that company leadership are most likely to fund.

Companies can share an in-focus graph with employees to signal the kinds of idea they are most likely to value. Far from feeling overly constrained, we've found employees appreciate the guidance and ideation is inspired (proving the adage "innovation loves constraints").

A common reaction to the in-focus graph is "doesn't this encourage incremental thinking?" The answer is not necessarily. Whether an idea is incremental or game-changing is orthogonal to whether the idea is strategically aligned. However, it is true that company leadership will need to explicitly encourage employees to think boldly in their ideation and not make off-limits ideas that would disrupt current products.

Figure 1: The In-focus graph

Ideas that align with mission and strategy but are not part of the short-term focus fall just outside the center. An example would be a product for the South African market but the short-term global expansion focus is starting with Latin America. As ideas move further away from the center of the graph, they are much less likely to be funded by company leadership. Or another way of thinking about it is the burden of proof gets higher as you move to the edge of the graph.

A product with traction may lose its funding for the following reasons:

- Change in strategy: While mission statements tend to rarely change, company strategies are updated much more frequently. New leadership, acquisitions, or business setbacks can all be triggers for significant changes in strategic direction. This means that a product that may have at one time in its journey have been in the center of the in-focus graph may fall out of alignment.
- Missing synergy: In the course of learning how to scale the business,

the company may learn that the product doesn't have synergy with the other products in the portfolio. For example, a company that sells all its products online discovers that their new product needs an enterprise sales force in order to scale. The company may decide it doesn't want to set up a whole new sales force for just this one product or feel that enterprise sales is outside its core competency.

- Prioritization: Sometimes it simply comes down to limited resources where all available funding has been allocated to other initiatives. The company leadership may feel that other products offer more promising growth prospects. Tough prioritization calls are a reality for almost every company.

The bottom line is once you have developed a formidable innovation engine, you can expect to have to make difficult decisions on what we'll call your "excess innovation".

Shutdown Pains

You might think having excess innovation is nirvana but having too much of a good thing presents a new set of challenges. Shutting down products will create problems for your innovation culture and potentially undermine the progress you've made.

For one, employees who have passionately working on an product that has customer validation and market traction will be thoroughly disappointed when that initiative is shut down. These employees, who will most often be your most valuable entrepreneurial talent will most likely not be happy to be reassigned to another project. At the very least, they are unlikely to apply the same passion to their new assignment. Worst case, they'll become cynical about innovating in the company and become a flight risk. We've observed several instances where a leader was delusional in his ability to keep disappointed employees engaged by getting them excited in his pet project.

Second, shutting down products with traction means disappointing the customers who are using that product. The fact that the product attained traction likely means there won't be good alternatives for those customers to use once the product goes away. Letting down what would not be an insignificant number of customers does erode goodwill and hurt the brand.

Third, shutting down products that have traction is a waste of the company's investment and a missed opportunity for growth if viable alternatives to exist.

Shutting down products may ultimately be inevitable. However, we believe you can make it a last resort instead of the first option when faced with excess innovation.

Excess innovation is not a hypothetical situation. Google and Intuit are two examples of companies that have successfully created formidable innovation engines based on empowered employees churning out great ideas. And while both companies are leaders at empowering intrapreneurs, we believe more could have been done to handle some of the successful products they decided to shut down.

Google has accumulated an impressive list of shutdown products. There is even a website called "Google Graveyard - A Resting Place for Great Ideas."[1] . One of the products in the graveyard is Google Reader, developed by engineer Chris Wetherell and launched in 2005 on Google Labs (their external portal for employees' 20% time projects). Reader made it easy for people to discover and keep tabs on their favorite websites. Reader graduated out of Labs in 2007 and went on to acquire several million active users. It was retired in 2013 as part of a wider "spring cleaning" with Google citing "while the product has a loyal following, over the years usage has declined."[2] The decision was not popular with customers who attempted in vain to persuade Google to keep Reader alive by collecting over 100,000 signatures on an online petition.

One of Intuit's successful Unstructured Time graduates was SparkRent, a service to make it easy for tenants to pay rent to their landlords electronically (at the time, over 70% of rents in the US were still paid by check). The service was launched in 2013 and acquired 10,000 active users. However, with the company narrowing its strategic focus, the service as shut down in 2015.

Even though both Google Reader and SparkRent had loyal customers and

---

[1] http://www.wordstream.com/articles/retired-google-projects

[2] https://googleblog.blogspot.com/2013/03/a-second-spring-of-cleaning.html

traction, the number of customers and revenue the services generated were miniscule on the scale of both companies' flagship offerings. Certainly both companies had to make difficult prioritization decisions. However, those decisions did not have to result in waste if they were equipped with a structured approach to handling excess innovation.

Managing Excess Innovation

If your company has a prolific innovation engine, we urge you to consider implementing an alternative to curtailing products with traction. What follows is a discussion of using an Emerging Products Division and the Spin-Along Approach for managing your excess of good ideas.

Emerging Products Division

Once you have a vibrant innovation culture that empowers employees to pursue their own ideas, you can expect employees will occasionally develop promising new products that may not be a fit with your existing business unit structure. Instead of allowing these products to fail because of lack of support from the business units, a company can set up an "Emerging Products Division" as a home for these orphan products. These orphan products can be restricted to H2 initiatives that have customer traction and are in the process of scaling. Over time, the emerging products that thrive and become H1s can be successfully integrated into an existing business unit or have a new business unit established for them.

Emerging products can provide valuable growth insurance if and when a company's current strategic focus runs out of gas by allowing companies to play in new markets. Stanford Graduate School of Business professor Charles O'Reilly states the key for company long term survival is to be ambidextrous: "It is the ability to simultaneously compete in mature markets where factors are customer intimacy, operational excellence, and incremental improvements, and to compete or explore new markets where the key factors to success are different, including flexibility and rapid adoption."[1]

IBM's Emerging Business Opportunity (EBO) approach is credited for helping IBM survive it's near death experience in the 1990s and reposition

[1]https://www.gsb.stanford.edu/insights/how-did-ibm-avoid-becoming-extinct

the company from a technology company to a business services organization.[1] There are a few challenges to consider with an Emerging Products Division. First, this division should not be perceived by employees as the "Innovation Division" responsible for all innovation in the company. The other business units will still be expected to innovate and develop new products that are a strategic fit.

Second, there may on occasion be conflicts between emerging products and mature products. Some new products may be competitive with existing products or cause sales channel confusion. We believe companies should resist the temptation to give business units veto power over emerging products. Instead, companies should exercise the mantra "if we're going to be disrupted, we'd rather disrupt ourselves." This requires that the Emerging Products Division be provided appropriate isolation and protection from the other business units.

The Spin-Along Approach

Many companies use corporate acquisitions as a means of entering new markets, acquiring new technologies or specialized talent ("acqui-hires"). For example, in the Prizmic story, the company purchased Makeni for the startup's mobile application. These "spin-in" venture activities are sometimes a tacit admission that certain innovations are more likely to succeed in a startup environment versus an established corporation. The thinking is that while a new product being developed is still in the early stages, it is likely to be crushed by the gravitational forces of the mature businesses in the enterprise before they are able to attain traction. Better to have that new product try to get traction in a more supportive startup environment. Once a startup has proven traction and a relatively significant customer base, it can be more successfully spun-in.

Conversely, companies may find they have developed technology or products for which they are unable to find a home in their business units can spin them out as a way of commercializing that investment.

René Rohrbeck, Mario Döhler, and Heinrich Arnold in their paper

---

[1] https://hbr.org/2012/07/exploring-and-exploiting-growt.html

"Combining spin-out and spin-in activities – the spin-along approach" [1] describe how Cisco and Deutsche Telekom Laboratories have combined spin-out and spin-in activities to what they call the "spin-along approach."

At Cisco, three engineers Mario Mazzola, Prem Jain, and Luca Cafiero have been involved in three separate spin-ins including Insieme Networks that Cisco funded and 21 months later purchased for $863 million. Insieme provided Cisco with a product in the important new Software-Defined Networking market.[2]

The spin-along approach can be utilized as a better alternative to simply shutting down a product that has market traction. In this case, the company will offer the product team the opportunity to spin-out with the product and provide seed funding with the expectation that the team will need to raise additional capital from elsewhere. The company will retain a right of first refusal as an option to spin-in the startup in the future. The product can now continue its journey instead of being curtailed with a possible upside for the company.

Of course there are a few challenges to consider with the spin-along approach. First, corporate acquisitions are notoriously prone to failure (studies showing that 70% to 90% of merger and acquisition activity destroy shareholder value). A company must develop strong competencies in integrating acquisitions if spin-ins become a regular part of their operating rhythm.

Second, spin-outs can be seen as greasing the path for a company's best employees to leave for the greener pastures of the startup world. We believe companies that have developed a strong innovation culture will still experience an exit of some of their best talent regardless especially after their pet product is shutdown. A company that has a good track record of spinning-out startups is likely to attract its unfair share of entrepreneurial minded employees. Also, you will discover that not all entrepreneurial employees will be choose to join a spin-out team, preferring the stability of the enterprise job.

---

[1] http://www.rene-rohrbeck.de/documents/Rohrbeck_Doehler_Arnold_(2007)_Spin-along-approach_paper.pdf

[2] http://www.businessinsider.com/why-cisco-showered-three-men-with-billions-2014-9

Third, when a startup is spun back in, those employees are likely not going to be eager to be back in the corporate environment. Like Milton James, the former CEO of Makeni in the Prizmic story, they may just be counting the days until they can cash out and leave. A fast-paced innovation culture will provide some mitigation. The spin-along approach also provides an appealing template for serial innovators to derive upside straddling between the startup and corporate worlds.

CHAPTER 10
THE AUTHORS' STORIES

Hugh Molotsi

I joined Intuit as a software engineer in 1993. My first product was QuickBooks for DOS. Working on a DOS application was not a glamorous choice for a young technologist because even though most personal computer users were still running the MS Disk Operating System, it was clear that MS Windows was the future. For me, joining an exciting and growing company as Intuit was the priority and working on DOS felt like a worthwhile compromise.

That first year on QuickBooks brought formative lessons that stayed with me the rest of my career. While I had been enamored by technology, I soon began to develop a stronger empathy for the users of our software. The stakes for successfully using our software were high for business owners. It could be the difference between staying in business or going out of business. It could enable the business to thrive and hire new employees, providing a livelihood for many more people. It could also mean the difference between a business owner going home to her family at 6pm versus staying up all night struggling with her books.

This empathy for customers was cultivated by an Intuit practice called "Follow Me Homes" where Intuit employees were encouraged to regularly visit customers in their homes and workplaces and observe how they were using our software. Follow Me Homes never failed at delivering new insights and reinvigorating the passion to make the software even better.

The nineties was also the time when the Internet was starting to take traction and become relevant to business applications. After working on Windows and Mac versions of QuickBooks, I had the privilege of being a part of a team that developed one of Intuit's very first Internet based services, Quicken Business Cashfinder. Even though Cashfinder eventually failed in market, it helped me realize a passion for building new businesses. This passion defined the rest of my 22 year career at Intuit and my entrepreneurial ventures today.

Insight

In 1999, after visiting several QuickBooks customers, I noticed that even though credit card use was becoming more prevalent, most small businesses we talked to didn't have a way of accepting credit card payments. I would ask why they didn't. The answers came down to one or more of the following: it was too expensive, too difficult, or they didn't know how to do it. A couple of small businesses even suggested that it would be great if Intuit would provide a solution!

The Challenge

Integrating credit card processing into QuickBooks was not rocket science. It helped that there were a number of companies that had developed virtual terminals which allowed you to process transactions on the web. All we needed to do is add a credit card option to the Receive Payments form in QuickBooks (which already had check and cash) and then send that data over a web connection to a partner who would do they heavier lifting of getting the transaction processed. We already had a couple of credit card gateway companies who were pleading to be Intuit's partner.

Convincing Intuit leadership that the idea was going to be easy was a more difficult challenge. Many leaders were convinced we were underestimating the complexity of the effort. We were already late in the yearly development cycle of QuickBooks and taking on an initiative like this didn't seem prudent. But after a number of meetings that didn't seem to go well at the time, we were able to win the support of a couple of key leaders who gave me and Scott Baird, a product manager, the green light to move ahead.

The Solution

After Scott and I vetted a number of prospective partners, we chose to partner with a few companies: Signio (a small startup eventually acquired by Verisign who would play the role of gateway), First Data (the big payments processor) and Wells Fargo (the merchant account bank). It turned out that the skeptical leaders were right—we had indeed underestimated all the complexities of creating this new service (yay for youthful exuberance!).

Integrating payments in QuickBooks was the easy part. For expedience, I created a COM object in Visual Basic to link QuickBooks to the gateway. Using Visual Basic was an inelegant approach but it eliminated the risk of having to make significant changes to QuickBooks late in the development cycle. In hindsight, I see now that my choice exemplified sound Lean Startup techniques - a Minimum Viable Product! We could rewrite the implementation in the next version of QuickBooks if the service was successful (which is what ended up happening).

The more difficult challenge was coordinating with partners who didn't always see eye-to-eye on our vision of how the service should work. We wanted an instant application process where the small business would find out right away if they were approved for a merchant account. We were assured it would take at least a week to complete the underwriting process (we settled for two days). We wanted to shorten the application from three pages to half a page of questions. We grappled with how to create a customer support experience where agents would be able to "hot transfer" customers to the appropriate partner when they had issues. When we would find bugs, partners would sometimes have to be convinced the problem was on their end.

Resolving many of these challenges required working through countless details. Tim Foy was assigned to be the program manager for the initiative and he was a lifesaver. He had the uncanny ability to anticipate issues and ask the right questions. For several weeks, we had daily 7 am PST calls, scheduled at a friendly time for our East coast partners, to hash out issues.

However, the biggest challenge we faced was that not everyone in the company was entirely supportive of our goal. For example, we had one documentation writer who was assigned to work with the team (we eventually had about a dozen team members by the time we launched). This writer was often difficult in meetings, questioning every decision and refusing to take action items. In my frustration, I decided to talk to her manager to see if she could encourage her employee to be more cooperative.

My meeting with the writer's manager will forever play in my memory. After I sat down in her office and explained why I wanted to see her, she completely laid into me. She said it was a bad idea to add credit card processing to

QuickBooks. We were a software company and have no clue about how to run a service like that. The whole thing was going to be a disaster for the company. Customers would be calling every day because their transactions weren't processed properly and we wouldn't know how to fix it. And on and on… (It turned out the hapless writer had just been doing her manager's bidding).

I was completely unprepared for this onslaught, having naively assumed I was going to get her help. Also, having just recently broken up with my girlfriend, I was in a very fragile emotional state. I sat there in stunned silence with the mantra playing in my head "don't cry, don't cry"! I'm proud to say that I was able to hold back the tears until I rushed out of the building and made it to the parking lot.

It turns out that while we had solid senior management support, many first-level and middle managers were not sold on what we were doing.

We were able to overcome these challenges and only 12 weeks after the project was kicked off, we launched the service.

The Results

At a small launch party to celebrate with our partners, Scott asked attendees to all predict how many customers we would get in the first year. Tim Knowlton from Wells Fargo predicted 300 customers. I predicted 30,000. Everyone else was somewhere in between. Tim and I were both way off. We would acquire approximately 3,000 customers that first year. I didn't realize it at the time, but we had achieved a great start for a brand new service. By 2003 we had 30,000 customers and the business looked so promising that Intuit purchased Innovative Merchant Solutions to replace Wells Fargo. As of 2015, Intuit Payments has over $100M revenue and 250K customers.

Reflection

The successful launch of the QuickBooks Merchant Account Service is one of the highlights of my career. Intuit generously awarded me it's first Founders Innovation Award in 2011 (my PM partner Scott would have also been awarded if he had still been at Intuit). I feel truly blessed to have gotten the opportunity. How many companies would entrust an engineer and product manager with that type of responsibility? This personal experience is a big reason why I am so passionate about empowering employees to be intrapreneurs. I know many other frontline employees have great ideas but don't have the same opportunity to bring them to life.

In fact, given that Intuit had no formal innovation program back in 1999, we were extremely lucky to overcome many of our obstacles. The lack of an incubative framework to help the whole company understand how to incorporate new products while mitigating risk would have gone a long way in bringing people along. Giving employees time and freedom avoids the impedance just to get simple experiments off the ground. Having a more collaborative culture encourages other employees with similar passions and complementary skills to chip in. We believe incorporating these facets into your innovation program means success doesn't have to rely so much on luck.

Jeff Zias

When I interviewed at Intuit in 2005 I didn't know what to expect.
A couple of my friends worked there and recommended I give it a shot.
Intuit had a strong reputation as a great employee-focused place to work. My friends loved working there, and the fact I had been an avid TurboTax user for years further increased my respect for Intuit.

I interviewed for an "initiative manager" role in the QuickBooks Payroll division. I showed up and interviewed with five different potential colleagues. A few days later I learned a job offer was coming from Intuit. Turns out they were looking for someone with startup experience, patents, and a focus on creativity and innovation. My unusual background and focus fit the bill.
I soon started and reported to Narinder Sandhu, the head of product development for QuickBooks Payroll. A month after starting Narinder sat me down to firm up goals for the year.

We wrote my projects and responsibilities across his whiteboard. Then he surprised me.

"We all have stretch goals, Jeff. What do you want your stretch goals to be?"

I had no idea, but we talked about the possibilities.

Narinder said "we're starting to look at this brand-new thing. It's called whitespace, we want to try to raise our employee engagement. Some of our execs went over to Google and were inspired about their 20% time. We want to see if a program like that could raise engagement. "

I had no idea what this whitespace thing was, but for some reason it sounded appealing. This was a thing Google was doing. And Google was super-cool. Also, this stretch goal addressed an enormous problem the division faced.

"Sure, tell me more," I said.

The Stretch Goal

Like many companies, we measured "employee engagement" yearly via survey. Employee engagement is meant to be a more meaningful measure than just employee satisfaction, which can be construed as a general appreciation of the job or company.

But employee engagement is defined as a mark of emotional commitment. Engaged employees truly care about their work and their company.

It turned out our employee engagement score was awful. Intuit always aimed to be world class on each measure, in this case a score of 85% or higher would be world class. 75% engagement was pretty mediocre. Our score, for the product development teams for QuickBooks Payroll, sat at 63%. The whitespace notion was this: if we told employees to spend 10% of their time being more self-directed, play with technology or whatever, perhaps this time and freedom would drive higher engagement.

I personally identified with the hypothesis that freedom, creativity, and self-directed activities could quickly raise engagement. I felt positive we would put some points on the board. But I suspected we may work hard for a year and raise the score 5%, making what could seem like minimal progress given the current abysmal score of 63%.

But my stretch goal was set: Use whitespace to raise our employee engagement.

So I started. It seemed to make sense to first walk around and talk with each of the 26 members of the department. That seemed like an approachable number of folks.

The Interviews

After talking with 3 engineers a pattern already emerged. In QuickBooks Payroll we worked towards a big yearly product release. And the code base was old and crusty. I learned that much of the giant QuickBooks codebase was 15 years old.

Engineers told us "It's old style C code. I keep working on this grungy code while my friends outside the company are doing web work and all sorts of cool stuff. I'm stagnating, stuck in this old codebase."

The Big Fail

After interviewing everyone it was clear we had an immediate opportunity. The freedom of whitespace could allow engineers to code in newer technologies. Engineers could practice new skills, learn new languages and platforms. They would break their shackles, coding beyond the digital dinosaur.

So we dove into crafting an email that Narinder sent out across the division. You have this whitespace time, 10% of your time to do cool things, go for it!"
We waited. The clock ticked. Days passed, then weeks.

We talked to folks. The results were clear - absolutely nothing was happening.

As root cause I heard "we're too busy, we have no time." And other thoughts came up - "that note you sent made no sense, skunkworks types of things never work, not here anyway, why even try?"

This critical and defeatist attitude surprised me. I had no idea what to try next.

The next Monday a young engineer on my team, Zach Moneypenny, showed up to our morning stand-up meeting and told us about an amazing weekend experience he had. He had attended the Yahoo Hack Day, and in his words, it was freakin' awesome.

"What did you do?" we asked.

Zach described the 24 hours of hacking, thinking, slamming snack foods and red bulls, through an all-nighter. The next day you get your 45 seconds to stand up with your laptop and demo your code to everyone. Zach was fired-up from the experience.

I asked a series of questions, how did they do it, what were the rules, who showed up, what structure, themes, which APIs?

We reached a quick conclusion. Let's try our own version of this!

We designed our version, and shifted many elements to better fit our culture. Our employees had no desire to pull all-nighters, to use-up the weekend, or to focus only on code (we wanted all functions to a take part). So we reshaped the hack day into more of an innovation day and set it for a weekday.

But what should we call it, it's not hack day really, right?

"Let's call it Hacktivism," Zach said.

The 'Quantum' Leap

The journey of a thousand miles begins with one step.
-Lao Tzu

We picked a date and put it on the Calendar. The invite went to every employee in the division. The VPs followed on with emails, please attend.

So our event, Hacktivism, hastily branded as a "sponsored by whitespace" activity, started to look tangible.

We reinforced the message please attend at staff meetings the weeks leading into the event.

The morning of Hacktivism came, and sure enough everyone showed up. We had lined-up a short kickoff with guest speakers. Our VP of Product Management, Terry Hicks, described what we knew about customer pains and opportunities in the payroll space.

On this fine spring day our ideas floated, were grilled, and then floated some more.

Grilled? We actually had a "process" in place called Idea Grill sessions. A volunteer would pitch their idea to the group, and the group would ask tough questions. Not a process for the thin-skinned. We grilled ideas from four volunteers in the middle of the day.

Our whole division was in attendance. The structure, social proof, and leadership support changed everything. Whitespace moved from fragile concept to reality.

At the end of the day each small team had written their idea out on the whiteboard and presented a 3 minute report to the crowd. Some engineers had already coded a bit.

This first Hacktivism was a success. Imperfect, small, but successful.

Soil had been tilled and a few (grass) seeds were now planted.

Victorious

On-going whitespace activity grew to a trickle and we began planning our second Hacktivism. We were invited to expand our program to invite the entire QuickBooks division. We were talking hundreds of people now at Hacktivism rather than dozens.

A few months later it was time to remeasure employee engagement in QuickBooks Payroll. I held my breath—employee engagement was now 83%. A 20 percentage point jump in just six months!

Not a person suspected coincidence.

Steps

Over the next eight years we went through the usual progression of innovation program maturity. At first we were almost entirely "event" based, for some of the reasons above. At first all we could do was ideation. At first we had trouble tying back to real customer needs.

But over time we upped our innovation game. We developed tools and "taste" for deepened customer empathy. Ideas started to strengthen, ties to customer-learning annealed. The program became official enough that we thought it needed a "real" name. We held an employee contest, and "Hacktivism" became "Idea Jams."

Then we deepened skills for prototyping and experimentation so ideas could iterate and improve.

Around this time, along with the set of colleagues who co-developed the Idea Jams across Intuit, I received a Scott Cook Innovation Award. This award is known as a prestigious recognition of innovation and impact at Intuit.

As the years went by we put dozens of more supportive programs in place. All the while employee engagement continued to rise.

Personal Take-aways

This experience marked the beginning of a new chapter in my life. My stretch goal had already turned into my favorite professorial endeavor "ever." I saw colleagues come alive, in new ways, with a simple activity.

My view of both Intuit and myself changed. I could plan and run a big "fun" event. Who knew? I coached people on how to participate, how to create, how to pitch an idea. I saw that activities like this led to fast change in the culture, and increasing engagement level of our entire division. I was, as they say, "Sold!"

And my God, if there were a chance to do this type of work full-time, then that would be a dream come true. I had never seen hearts and minds transform so quickly.

That day in 2006 I believed we saw and began living the key to great work. I believe that today. In my mind, as rudimentary as it was, the elements of Idea Jams describe the keys to thriving organizations of the future.

I didn't believe in magic, still don't. But, as Norman Peale said, "imagination is the true magic carpet ride." Employees bringing their fun, imaginative, creative, true selves into work to collaborate and innovate puts all of us on this magic carpet.

So allow us to craft, together, the Magic Carpet Factory.

KEY RESOURCES
FOR INTRAPRENEURSHIP

Artifacts for your Intrapreneurial Journey

The journey to building a culture of innovation at a company requires that you develop several resources to engage the organization. This section includes resources referenced in the Prizmic story. They are based on real artifacts we have used during our time leading innovation. We offer them to you here as what we hope are helpful starting points on your journey. Consider these "open source" and feel free to use them in your own company and make improvements as you apply them.

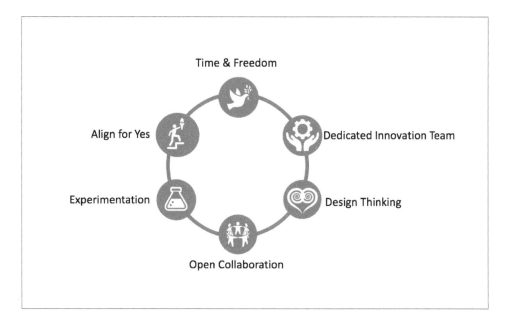

Time & Freedom Key Resources

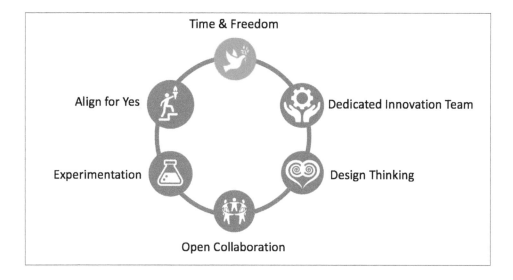

Resource: The Whitespace Time Announcement

Hi folks,

By now you may have heard rumblings about the new "employee autonomy" program we want to launch in the Consumer division. We're calling this program whitespace time, and we think it's going to be a win for everyone. We're excited to put the announcement of this program launch in writing. Here is some of how this came about and how we're going to implement it.

In the past month, we've been engaging in many conversations with employees to discuss how we can make Prizmic an even better place to work. One of the consistent themes that emerged is this: We have great people with great ideas, but we provide limited time or freedom to pursue those ideas. In benchmarking several best practice companies, we saw that time and freedom was built into their approach and culture (e.g. Google, Apple, 3M, W.L. Gore, etc.). In our desire to create an environment where people get a chance to pursue their ideas for improving the business or our environment, we have set out to address four key areas:

1. Clearing time for autonomy by asking you to use up to 10% of your time as "whitespace"
2. Building this whitespace into the work schedule, thereby allowing employees to be more innovative
3. Providing more opportunity for uninterrupted work - in order to be more productive
4. Provide an opportunity to work on projects of your choice that you believe will:
   a. Create new innovative solutions for customers, or
   b. Make our internal processes and tools better, or
   c. Help you learn important new skills

The first steps to achieving these goals is a set of actions that we are going to launch on October 13th. Then we'll learn together as a team. These ideas were provided by employees who have helped us tackle these opportunities together

-

- No Meeting Fridays: Effective October 13th, there will be no meetings scheduled after 11:30 on Friday.
    - To ensure you get the most out of your time for innovation, work/code environment improvement, or professional development, you may want to choose to use the uninterrupted free time for these purposes.
    - Or you can choose different time for your personal project and use Friday afternoon to do uninterrupt work on your current deliverables.

The approach will be simple and lightweight... think about the ideas, improvements or concepts you are most passionate about. Feel free to speak with your manager to fully engage their support ... everything from hashing out ideas and unblocking your way to providing encouragement.

Ideas that have been surfaced by others thus far include:

- New Product Ideas
- Refactoring code
- Getting closer to customers (adopting a customer, blogging,...)
- Learning new technology or new professional skills
- Immersive workshops and sessions with peers

In doing this, we are asking each team to define a process for sharing your learnings...for example, a forum where you discuss your learnings or new product ideas with your team.

Prizmic is our place of work, our professional lives. We all know the projects we work on take a huge amount of work on everyone's part to deliver. However, we've heard from many of you, and have felt ourselves, that we are out of balance on how we are spending our time. While we understand that creativity cannot be prescribed and does not happen on certain schedules, we believe that if we create this space and time that we all respect for individual expression and creativity then great things will happen to improve our customers' lives and our lives as employees.

We don't want to get more prescriptive than this and encourage you to be creative with how you use and "discover" the time. But, if you have any questions, don't hesitate to ask your manager or any of the leaders.

Thank you for all your amazing work and we look forward to an even more amazing future together. We've only just begun...

- Rowan and the Prizmic Whitespace Task Force

Resource: The Hack Day Sign Up Form

Prizmic "Accelerate our Journey to the Cloud" Hack Day Registration -
Your Name and Contact Information

Please enter one registration record per team, with the team lead filling-in this "Your name and contact..." section

First Name * _____
Last Name * _____

Select the 'name' of the Hack Day track you are registering for

Tracks:
- ☐   1. Cloud services/computing, end-user facing
- ☐   2. Cloud infrastructure enablement
- ☐   3. Tools to accelerate the journey (internal tool, processes or program innovations)
- ☐   4. Not yet decided (which is OK!)

Tell us the category of "award" you are up for:
- ☐   Prior work in-play (if you have been working along in Whitespace on the idea already)
- ☐   One day sprint (if you are first starting at this Hack Day)

Your Idea
Idea Description (<140 characters)

_____

Location info:
Palo Alto __ Phoenix __ Boston __ Delhi ___ Austin ___

Email Address
_____

Your "Team"
(If it is just you and you would like to meet people there, just fill it out with your name)
If you have a team, just submit one entry, but please list your team members here

Names of my team members
_____

Team Name (optional)
Prizm-DB record link: for describing your idea in our company repository (optional)
_____

Resource: How to Run an Effective Hack Day

From: Whitespace Time Champions
To: All Prizmic Employees
Subject: Running Great Hack Days
Hi All,
Proper, systematic execution of "Hack Days fundamentals" is now more important to us than ever. Like we've seen, well planned and executed Hack Days foster creativity, enable sky-high engagement, and drive exciting results. That "results" part is what we've got to be all about.

The key to running a great Hack Day need to become one of the central capabilities here at Prizmic. And some of the keys to reinforce are:

1. Great Hack Days **frame for focus** . Innovation loves constraints. But many Hack Days leave everything open, blue sky.

    Well-run Hack Days lay out specific themes and goals. A recent Quora question was "What is the coolest theme for a Hack Day." The question's most up-voted answer was "Augmented reality." In this example, the Hack Day narrowed scope to a single technology-based target.

    Other approaches also apply constraints by limiting the customer problem space. At Intuit, we held a set of a Hack Days focused on "increasing the financial capability of youth." Teams constrained their thinking within this specific problem domain. In turn, this focus helped generate more relevant ideas.

2. Great Hack Days **Set scope** . Most teams will try to do too much given the allotted time. Design your Hack Days to make as many participants successful as possible. How is the event helping participants to establish the proper scope? Helping participants

narrow is often a key. For example, one way of guiding is asking engineers to "focus on a technical Leap of Faith. What is single most important thing for your code to prove? How will you prove this as inexpensively as possible?" And Sometimes describing the "myth-busting" metaphor helps. "What is the key myth you are trying to bust?"

3. Great Hack Days **cajole with coaching** . It's fine to think of participants as big boys and girls who don't need coaching. Few are looking for "authorities" to be walking around, telling them what to do. Yet, many participants could use the help. In many areas, skilled mentors are available, ready to come over and help. Why not sign up folks to help transform mediocre teams into excellent teams?

4. Great Hack Days **Provide pizazz.** Hack Days can be engaging, impressive, full of great ideas. Attendees generally do better when they are pushed to be less incremental, more bold, more risk-taking. Teams need to be pushed towards novelty and creativity. Otherwise, the outcomes may be nothing more than a sea of "meh." "

5. Great Hack Days **Concentrate on customers.** If the Hack Day is purely focused on technology or capabilities, fine. Just be explicit about that. But often the theme addresses real needs faced by end-users or society. In this case, it is almost a "sin" to not encourage customer-focused innovation practices. Design thinking, empathy for customers, and rapid experimentation will be helpful to the participants.

    Organizers need to encourage customer-back "how might we find and solve well for a customer" thinking.

    For bonus points, customers should be recruited for the event. Having customers available for empathy activities and rapid experimentation adds a key new dimension.

6. Great Hack Days **Vet a Venue.** First thing, lock in the venue. Locking down key resources for a Hackathon isn't easy. Nailing down the proper venue can be the most challenging logistic of all.

If you fail to plan and must fall back to a lousy venue, good luck. People are sensitive to the look, feel, and vibes attached to your venue. Your attendees need room to move, places to sit, bathrooms, lighting, and water. Also, do not forget power strips!

7. Great Hack Days **Enable everyone** . Hack Days can cover any topic. The themes don't need to be product focused. For example, an HR department can run a Hack Day focused on programs that on-board employees in a more delightful manner. And smart Hack Days pull together small cross-functional teams. It takes all sorts of skills to ideate, make things, design, and build. Team members can also talk to customers and explore alternative ideas while engineers build.

   If the Hack Day is one that only focuses on the software coding aspect, then the organizers must be clear about that. Otherwise they'll confuse and disappoint folks.

8. Great Hack Days push **Humility over Hype.** Some Hack Days seem to encourage teams to pitch hype. A more powerful approach is to ask teams to humbly seek solutions to big customer problems. The best approach for teams is to "speak" the language of customer needs. Describing an unmet customer need and how the innovation may solve it well is a strong approach.

9. Great Hack Days **enable experimentation.** Hack Days work best when participants focus on fast learning, with an experimentalist's mindset. Other people may focus on hyping their amazing breakthrough innovation. Instead, teams can articulate what they need to learn, how they will learn it. The true goal of the team should be to develop stronger evidence that their solution is workable.

10. Great Hack Days **Jettison judging** . HIPPOs stands for (HI)ghest (P)aid (P)erson's (O)pinion. The only problem is that HIPPOS are often wrong. The smartest people in the world are often wrong. Especially when it comes to innovations in the nascent stages. So you must instead work to save the judges from themselves.

Maybe you desire judges so you can award teams. Your desire to recognize great teams and give out prizes is understandable, even honorable. To award and recognize teams in a productive manner, it's simple: Bring in customers and ask them give feedback. That feedback can be channeled into recognition and prizes for participating teams.

It does no good for leaders to appear in front of everyone as "HIPPOs", judging ideas based on their personal preference. Much better for all parties involved is a focus on getting close to customers. Done right, the feedback from customers can more deeply engage employees in the Hack Day while giving them more experience in deeply understanding what customers care about.

11. Great Hack Days **Finish fantasticly**. The Hack Day is not a rock concert, but it only makes common sense to plan to end on a high note. Finish with energy, music, speakers with big subwoofers, quick demos, short summations, and applause.
Great Hack Days leave folks energized, fulfilled, and wanting to come back for more.

12. Great Hack Days **Intend to improvise.** So it is game time, and you've done a fantastic job of planning. Your detailed google-doc checklist would make the Joint Chiefs of Staff green with envy Yet something happens and your plan goes to hell.
Well of course, this is life on earth, $%&! is going to happen When the inevitable strikes, be a natural improviser. Work with your core team to find a solution, and fast. Have the reflexes of a cat, the instincts of a jazz musician, and the brains of a speed-chess champion.

13. Great Hack Days **Furnish Food (fine, fun food!)**
The small stuff really isn't small. Don't skimp on food and beverages

And for God's sakes remember coffee ... lest you create a zombie patrol of headache-laden monsters of negativity.

Other key details include power, solid WiFi, prizes and cool giveaways. Also remember chairs, tables, microphones & screens (if big demos happen at any point).

14. Forge the fun. Hold a planner's huddle with your core team before

     kick-off. Get everyone in a good mood, tell jokes, pump each other up and spread the wealth. Your Hack Day is best served with optimism, energy, playfulness, warmth, and FUN!

Alright everyone, happy hack-daying! Let us know if you need any help, what you've tried, what you've learned.

Best,
The Whitespace Time Champions

Template: Prizmic Net Promoter Survey for Hack Days

From: Carol Jacobs
To: Whitespace_Time_Taskforce
Subject: PLEASE REVIEW: Let's use this Net Promoter Survey after every Hack Day or Jam or whatever!

Hey Team,
Although we know we are entirely awesome and virtually perfect people, we do need to measure how well our Hack Days actually work for attendees :-) Let's validate our awesomeness is all I'm saying.

I'm proposing we use the fairly well known Net Promoter Survey approach to understand how well we've done. If you're not familiar, in a nutshell, the Net Promoter Score (NPS) was developed as away of finding out if a product or service was developing customer loyalty. And if customers are truly loyal, it means they're kinda loving on what you do.

Many of the top companies in the world like Apple, Vanguard, Verizon, and American Express are big advocates of NPS. I always like to be in good company friends, how about you?

Why do this?

We need to commit to continuous improvement. Gathering Net Promoter feedback after each engagement with our "customers" - the employees we serve - engagement with us, we can see opportunities and then take action.

How do you run a Net Promoter Survey?

NPS is calculated asking customers what has been referred to as the "ultimate question": "on the basis of your experience with Y (usually a company product or an experience), how likely are you to recommend X to your friends or colleagues?"

Customers are asked to select a score within the range 0 (Not at all likely) to 10 (Extremely likely). Responses are then bucketed into the following segments:

- 0-6 are considered Detractors
- 7-8 are considered Neutral
- 9-10 are considered Promoters

NPS = % Promoters – % Detractors

The magic of NPS is thought to be the idea that detractors are a big deal. They have a lot to do with success, or lack thereof, and need to be heavily weighted.

The recommendation from SAT Metrics, one of the developers of NPS, is to follow the

a promoter (0-10) question with a question about the key drivers for promotion and for detraction, giving customers pre-defined options to select from. Then the next question can be an open question with a free text field for the answer. This allows you to collect a pure "voice of the customer"

The power of the survey is also based on the study of outcomes versus feelings. Customer Satisfaction is a "perception metric". NPS is an "Outcome metric", where the user reports what they are going to do, not how they feel.

And what does the score mean?

A score above +70% score is considered world class. It's possible to score as low as -100%. Let's not suck!

Proposed NPS survey for Hack Days

1. How likely are you to recommend attending a Hack Day to your colleagues?

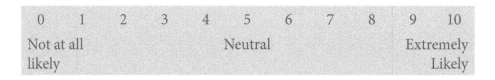

0	1	2	3	4	5	6	7	8	9	10
Not at all likely					Neutral				Extremely Likely	

2. What were the key drivers for your rating? (check all that apply)
   - Resources
   - Topic
   - Energy
   - Rate of progress

3. Why did you give the rating you did above?

   _____

Check it out folks. Send me your feedback. As always, let's have fun and do this thing!

-Carol

Resource: The Whitespace Time Survey

Intro and Survey Questions

This survey intends to understand your experience with Whitespace time and how this program can be improved. Please think of your Whitespace time experiences in the context of the ongoing 10% of time allocated for employees to pursue projects of personal interest, as well as events such a Jams, Hack Days/Weeks, and incubation sessions.

1. Which segment or group do you work in? (Please check all that apply)

- ☐ Consumer
- ☐ Enterprise
- ☐ Mobile
- ☐ Global

2. What functional area do you work in?

- ☐ Engineering
- ☐ Quality Assurance
- ☐ User Experience Design
- ☐ Product Management
- ☐ Finance
- ☐ HR
- ☐ Technology Infrastructure
- ☐ Other (please specify)

3. Over the past 6 months, how much Whitespace Time did you use?

☐ None
☐ Less than 10 hours
☐ Between 10 and 40 hours
☐ More than 40 hours

4. If you tend to use Whitespace Time on a particular day of the week, which day?
☐ NA, no particular day
☐ Friday
☐ Thursday
☐ Wednesday
☐ Tuesday
☐ Monday
☐ Other? _____

5. Please describe how frequently and for how long you use Whitespace Time? For example: *"Every other Friday, all day"*, or *"Usually afternoons for roughly 2 hours, Tues and Thursday"*, etc.
Your description: _____

6. If you are using Whitespace Time, what are you working on? (Please check all that apply)

☐ Improving an existing area of functionality
☐ Solving a new customer problem
☐ Running lean experiments
☐ Making our code or work environment better
☐ Innovating at a Hack Days (or similar event)
☐ Professional development (learning new technologies or skills, etc.)
☐ Other (please specify) _____

7. When you use Whitespace Time, is it usually:

- ☐ Alone
- ☐ Working as part of a small group
- ☐ Other _____

8. If you're not using much Whitespace Time, could you tell us why?

_____

9. How likely are you to recommend use of the Whitespace time program to another employee?

0	1	2	3	4	5	6	7	8	9	10
Not at all likely					Neutral					Extremely Likely

What are the primary reasons for this rating?

_____

10. What would make Whitespace Time better for you, or your projects, or Prizmic as a whole?

_____

Resource: Key Performance Indicators - Useful Innovation Metrics for Whitespace Time

Key success metrics type	Customer: employees	Customer: end-users
Positive word of mouth	• Number of employee referrals/shares made regarding Whitespace Time • Net promoter score of Whitespace Time	• Number of customer referrals/shares made from the service or offering that emerged from Whitespace Time • Net promoter score of the service or offering that emerged from Whitespace Time
Ease of use	• Total time from team's idea formation to testing the idea with customers • Percentage of teams that "'stall out'" during experiment release workflow	• A custom measurement. *Ease* as defined for the specific app/service/feature that emerged from Whitespace Time
Delivered customer benefit	• Percentage of employees with Whitespace Time ideas releasing experiments • Percentage of employee that are able to pursue an idea they care about	• Another custom measurement: each app/service defines the key customer value and measures to what extent the customer derives the value. Teams cannot be considered successful if they don't deliver the benefit!

Frictionless experimentation	• Number of total Whitespace Graduates • Number of Whitespace Time projects that start up • Percentage of Whitespace ideas that become graduates • Number of Hack Days • Time from new whitespace idea to 'graduate'	• Percentage of actively used apps that are whitespace graduates
Active use	• Percentage of employees regularly using Whitespace Time • Frequency of employee's use of Whitespace Time	• Number representing active customer use as defined per app/ product/service emerging from Whitespace Time

Resource: Making Time for Innovation

From: Boris

To: Whitespace_Catalysts

Subject: Tactics for Time

To maximize our success, we know we need to afford our Prizmicers time to tap into their passion. But we also know people are super busy! Just telling people to manage their time better doesn't seem to help much.

What if we outline specific tactics for employees at all levels to allocate time for thinking, innovation, and being more free-thinking?

Key Time and Freedom Tactics

Interstitial

Teams generally have peaks and valleys of effort and intensity. Our teams either work in agile sprints or work towards project deadlines off the old Gantt chart. In either case, the team stays heads-down for some amount of time but comes up for air after ending a sprint or reaching a milestone. A best practice is to schedule free-time for jamming, ideation, or hackathons at these points. For example, my friend Alan at Intuit told me this one: Intuit's QuickBooks product team went heads-down for a six month period working hard towards their fall product release deadline. As soon as the product was shipped, they took their well-planned and well-deserved Unstructured Time in the form of a full, contiguous week. And note: the team ended up building a mobile version of QuickBooks!

Periodic

Many teams find success setting up the Hack Days or "jammin" time at quarterly, monthly or weekly intervals. Just the act of putting something on the calendar can create the light structure and implied permission to enable free thinking and innovative results. For example, Facebook recently ran their 50th large Hackathon, and these periodic events are sent from the calendar of CEO Mark Zuckerberg.

Baked-in

A powerful technique is to build or bake the time into project plans. For example, software company Atlassian has a 20% time program and follows the agile process for development teams. For each agile sprint, the scrum master makes sure a 20% "chunk" of time is placed into each team member's backlog. In this way, the time for thinking, dreaming, risk-taking and innovating becomes baked into the plan.

Buddy-system

Some people need a running or workout buddy. Finding a partner can forge the commitment needed to lock in the time and build the habit of usage. Eddie Lucero and KC Liew are two engineers who work in Intuit's ProConnect division. Soon after they began working together, Eddie and KC identified a shared passion for building new technologies that make accountant's workflow faster and easier. Over the past couple of years they joined every 10% Unstructured Time Jam and contest they could, and have delivered a handful of new features that make accountant's lives easier. Their impromptu "buddy system" allows them to bounce ideas of one another, inspire each other to persevere, cover for each other when the buddy temporarily goes under-water, and stay focused on innovating for accountants.

Grand Challenge Contests

Great leaders issue grand challenges. For example, if you work for an online store your CEO may have issued you a challenge like -

"Deliveries currently take a whole week! How might we reduce that delivery time to 1 day ... or 1 hour?"

These grand challenges generally have a start date, a set of milestone dates and a finish date or "recognition" milestone. The challenge structure helps employees plan their time allocation. Motivated employees form small teams and work at their own pace to address the grand challenge. At Intuit, over a dozen large Innovation Contests have been held, resulting in hundreds of active challenge teams, hundreds of engaged employees, and the eventual delivery of important new features, tools, processes and offerings.

Employing these best practices can help ensure that your programs to give employees time and freedom are not perceived cynically but instead produce value and consistent utilization.

Dedicated Innovation Team Key Resources

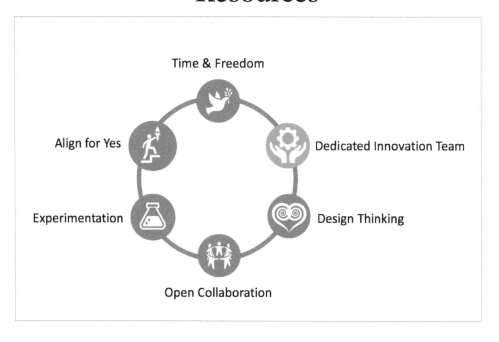

Resource: The Whitespace Catalysts Proposal

To: Sebastian@Prizmic.com

From: Patty Porter

Subject: Our CEO Staff Presentation, Whitespace Catalysts Proposal Doc

Hi Sebastian,

Here is a soft copy of the proposal we discussed.

Best,

Patty, Tyrone, and Boris

Prizmic Whitespace Catalysts Proposal

Overview

Whitespace Time is allowing Prizmic employees to tap into their passion to drive growth. We have seen a good deal of activity and results from Whitespace Time, but we've identified a number of obstacles to Whitespace Time success. We intend to do better for this important program.
This proposal examines how we are doing, what external lessons can be applied to our journey, and what we propose as next steps.

Current State

Whitespace Time started as an experiment within the Enterprise division. In January it became a formal program, driven company-wide by our Whitespace Time taskforce.

Whitespace Time is not meant to only increase employee engagement. The desire is for Whitespace Time to help Prizmic reach top priority business goals. For example, Voice-it, an offering that graduated from Whitespace Time, currently drives 30% of Enterprise Division revenue.

We feel that Whitespace Time is also an employee culture program. It relates directly to our Prizmic values, and how those values work to define the innovative culture that will enable us to reach our aggressive goals.

Specifically, the Prizmic values speak to a culture of innovation and the kind of time and freedom employes can use, particularly when we look at:

- **Courage:** Solve big customer problems, think beyond what is accepted as possible
- **Passion:** Be fired up, Inspire with your insights and energy
- **Experimentation:** Lead with a hypothesis, savor the surprises
- **Bias for action:** Act, learn and choose what we will and will not do
- **Teamwork:** Team-up, be boundaryless, and drive smart action
- **Excellence:** Delight our customers and partners with experiences they love

We have seen evidence that the time and freedom associated with Whitespace Time allows employees to feel more engaged, live the Prizmic values more deeply, and then drive both personal and corporate growth.

So how are we doing?

Whitespace Time is currently up and running in our key divisions. We have major gaps in consumer and customer care where, given busy schedules and lack of formal support Whitespace Time is unhealthy.

Internal Evidence Whitespace Time Works

Some select innovator's quotes on programs, tools and products that came from Whitespace Time:

- Voice-it - "Voice-it quickly became our top selling service, and I've never seen team members, or Prizmic Board of Director members for that matter - so excited!" - Lindsey Badal, GM
- Piped Lists - "Who knew this simple HTML/CSS list component would now be used in 50% of our products, we're bursting with pride." - Srivinas Bhatia, software engineer, consumers
- Lean-Out - "This leadership program from HR is the highest rated training in the company, bar none. That's what passion for a cool idea does." - Kristin Gabriel, Leadership Development Specialist

- Tiempo Front-End - "The Prizmic Tiempo front end re-architecture was Whitespace Time to begin with. That enabled our complete rewrite and the whole mobile platform, a breakthrough." - Laurence Castle, Architect, central platform dev

Challenges

Employee verbatims on Whitespace Time:

Whitespace Time is for product teams, not for functional teams and organizations, like HR or Finance, that don't work on end-user facing products"

- "It only drives engagement, not growth"
- "This wastes time by letting people go off in crazy, useless directions"
- "Leaves teams high and dry, with no resources and no chance of support"
- "The program doesn't need support, the program will happen 'naturally'"
- "It's not even discussed in my work group"
- "Working 80 hours a week there is no time to have Whitespace Time"

On the positive side:

- "It drives innovation and employee engagement"
- "By allowing me to use Whitespace Time, I've been able to come up with solutions to age long problems because I was given a chance to focus on something I am crazily passionate about"
- "We get to work on projects that we are passionate about, that help Prizmic and its customers, but that do not necessarily fall directly into our job descriptions! It's very energizing"
- "It's the way we innovate."
- "I heard about Whitespace TIme and joined Prizmic. 'Nuff said!"

We chose to interview more employees and drill down on two areas: lack of awareness and manager-leader resistance. -

Lack of awareness

HR has been reluctant to put Whitespace Time back into the orientation program since there is so much on-boarding info to cover, and Whitespace Time (chicken and egg problem) may not be used in the group the employee is joining.

Some forms of awareness building -
- Whitespace Time leaders in BU/FGs
- Articles in Prizmic pubs
- Brown bag presentations, other blogs, activities

Manager-leader Resistance

In some cases the leader didn't personally believe in the value of Whitespace Time. In most cases where resistance formed, the lack of available seemed to hurt the most.
- Show the value with more success stories
- Help see how people can find the time with Hack Days, working it into product backlogs, etc.
- Emphasize CEO-down support for the priority of this and innovation

Benchmarking

We've found a large body of external secondary research showing that giving employees time and freedom raises engagement while improving worker creativity and productivity [T. Amabile et al, see section 3].

Additionally, some of the most innovative and engaging companies use time and freedom programs to inspire innovation and high employee engagement.

Company	Qualifications	How
Google	Fortune #1 innovation company, #1 Best Company to work for	50% revenue comes from 20% time derived products. Now also trying Google X model
GORE Creative Technologies Worldwide	Perennial best company to work for, most innovative company, high engagement, double digit growth	High freedom, no job titles, all associates innovate, 10% dabble time for all employees
Adobe	Forbes 2015 most innovative company,	Kickbox program, thousands of employees opt-in with new entrepreneurial ideas
Atlassian	40% year to year growth, heralded in Fortune, forbes, HBR, etc	Ship-it day hackthons, 20% time, every employee innovates, high autonomy
3M	Perennial most innovative company, double digit growth	Freedom, 15% rule, recent new to world prod revenue metric, genesis grants

Here's a little more information about what these companies specifically do:

Google

Google has 9 principles of innovation
1. Innovation comes from anywhere
2. Focus on the user
3. Aim to be ten times better
4. Bet on technical insights
5. Ship and iterate
6. Give employees 20 percent time
7. Default to open processes
8. Fail well
9. Have a mission that matters

3M

Innovation Culture
High Freedom - "everyone innovates". "we expect everyone to be zeroed-in on these behaviors:"

Play to win; Prioritize and execute; Innovation;

Foster collaboration and teamwork; Develop others and self; Act with integrity and transparency

Key levers: "This is how we look at fostering and supporting this culture of innovation. It's really a part of our DNA."[8]

Freedom of expression and thought; "Every employee gets 15% free time, which we call the 15% culture; to enable new ways to explore and discover what's new. It teaches leadership and new skills, it also fosters the pursuit of the next big idea. Many of our new products have come from this 15% culture."

Adobe

Innovation Culture
John Warnock and Chuck Geschke – "… **good ideas come from everywhere in the company**, and that it's important to create new markets rather than being a 'fast follower.'"

That spirit of risk-taking and innovation has touched every part of Adobe, from major business model shifts to cutting-edge research and product innovations.

Levers

Kickbox program – Opt in, get a box that guides you to innovate, and go from red box to blue box where you get $1000 and freedom to experiment and spend …

founders believe every employee can opt in to freely innovate, rapid prototyping focus

W.L. Gore

100 Best companies to work for in the US, Fortune magazine, one of only 5

companies on the top 100 list every year since 1984

Innovation Culture

1. Fully democratized, everyone is an "associate"
2. Everyone innovates
3. Focus on customer back innovation
4. These are made up of belief in the individual, in small teams, all in the same boat and holding a longer term view as the payoff but not sacrificing the short-term gain. - See more at <u>Innovation excellence, on WL Gore</u> …

Levers

- 10% dabble time for every employee
- They practice a "lattice" network structure connecting every individual in the organization to every other

Commonalities of these top innovation companies:

Here's our hypothesis: The great results these benchmarked companies continuously achieveme come from a culture rich in employee freedom, time to think and innovate, and a deep appreciation of collaborative experimentation.

Challenges

1. How do we create a culture that drives amazing, continuous improvement to the benefits delivered to customers?
2. How might we turn every employee into an informed, confident, and energized innovation dynamo?
3. How do we help our leaders balance the different types of work required to deliver for short term (execute our existing businesses) and long term (discover new opportunities).

Proposed Plan
New annual plan and key levers

1. New innovation micro-portal for Prizmic innovation stories
2. Evaluating "Mural" tool for small innovation team collaborative experimentation
3. Catalyze an expanding community of people using Whitespace Time and sharing their results
4. Rapid Prototyping workshops, coaching and training
5. Societal focus, CSR innovation, Shared Value and Innovation team partnership
6. Building the case, with data, for stronger leadership support of grassroots innovation

Whitespace Time Leadership
A culture of time and freedom for employees to innovate

- **Shared Outcome:** All employees are autonomous, innovative, know the Prizmic values, and drive innovative breakthroughs for customers.
- **Success Metrics:**
  - An increasing number of new "grassroots" ideas that graduate to fully supported new features, tools, services, products and offerings.
    - # of graduates/quarter
    - Leading metric, "autonomy score", %0-100 for each division
- **Work to Be Done:**
  - Whitespace Time Catalyst Community:
    This program will allow us to build increasing levels of capability to organize and coach Prizmic employees, driving freedom & time programs to increase innovation that is tied directly to top strategic priorities ...
    - Driver: Boris,
    - Approvers: Patty, Sebastian,
    - Contributors: Carol, Org leaders like Sara, Kyle, David, Katherine, Michael, Lori, Melissa and more;
    - Informed: Selected teams using the Whitespace Time program

Resource: The Prizmic Labs Proposal

To: Sebastian@Prizmic.com
From: Patty Porter
Subject: Our CEO Staff Presentation, Labs Proposal Doc
Hi Sebastian,

Here is a soft copy of the proposal we discussed.

Best,

Patty, Tyrone, and Boris

Prizmic Labs Proposal
Current State

Prizmic has the opportunity to drive faster growth. A team dedicated to helping the company realize the "press release" vision below (a vision of fast growth) is needed. Without dedicated support for innovation, our company – like any large, successful company – will fall prey to the Innovator's Dilemma.

Without innovation, Prizmic will fail to grow.

A dedicated team of innovation drivers can work to help the company dramatically increase benefits delivered to customers. This can be achieved by developing and delivering powerful innovation capability.
methods and programs like:

- **Value delivered to customers:** We teach the mindset and methods related to understanding and delivering more value, faster.
- **Design Thinking training**: We teach the concepts of design thinking to a growing set of enthusiastic employees. Employee

become well versed in applying Design Thinking to their jobs. The training focuses on priorities of deeply understanding our current and future customers, brainstorming to develop broad sets of solution possibilities, and rapidly experimenting to establish what truly solves well for customers.

- **Rapid Prototyping/Experimentation**: This particular skill, a subset of Design Thinking, helps employees get close to customers, go broad, and harvest surprises and insights.
- **Prizmic Labs Catalysts**: We take the most enthusiastic and skilled design thinkers and build our growing army of highly-skilled innovation coaches.
- **Whitespace Time**: Volunteer leaders across the company encourage and coach grassroots innovation via Jams, Innovation Days, challenges and innovation contests.
- **Metrics for Innovation**: "What you measure is what you do." Companies live and die by this 'metrics sword.' So we work to reimagine, re-design and hone this sword.
- **Change Initiatives:** Through important channels like CEO staff offsites, company-wide Jams and Forums, we introduce and teach new mindsets and skills to leaders across Prizmic.

Challenges

In rolling out new ways of working, particularly new innovative ways of working, we've seen a number of obstacles and challenges pop up. By listing these challenges our plan to win can become better informed.

Lack of awareness

Despite the progress made socializing concepts like design thinking, a large percentage of Prizmic employees still have little understanding of innovation best practices.

Lack of Training

Every year, 150 new employees join Prizmic. Design thinking training isn't offered as part of employee on-boarding. We hire new senior leaders who are

Model: We use these mechanisms ourselves. In doing so, we deepen our understanding of the tools, principles and mindsets we wish to teach. Then we refine and improve the teachable and coachable aspects of each one.

Teach: We work to teach our system of innovation to employees. We believe the right training increases the innovation capability of employees. Great results follow.

To understand what is truly needed, we look at the current state of what is happening with innovation at Prizmic -

In many areas around Prizmic, innovation is thriving. Teams are applying the innovation best practices to drive outstanding outcomes. Examples come from teams creating services for use inside the company, and from teams creating offerings for external customers. We have employees who are passionate advocates and practitioners of Prizmic's innovation methodology. This passion is exemplified with dozens of events and innovation activities held across the company each year.

Some divisions of the company already apply best practices. But uptake of these practices is at best spotty. Some employees use design thinking, Whitespace time, innovation jams. These divisions also encourage teams to run experiments and achieve the succession metrics.

Methods and programs which have proven to be successful here in the past...
- Customer-focused visionary innovation
- Innovation coaches and facilitators
- Employee freedom and time
- Jams, Hackathons
- Outside influences and inspiration
- Whitespace Time leaders across the company

also not familiar with our innovation methods. As one Prizmic team member put it, "If you can't identify the bat or the ball, you probably can't play baseball very well."

A related issue is that since leaders are not trained, they cannot coach teams to consider the elements of design thinking. They don't know what they don't know.

Relationship to Daily Work

Our core product teams do not all operate in the same manner. Some innovation methods are practiced in short-lived sprint sessions. Often teams will "do a one-off design" session rather than apply the principles within the context of an ongoing development process.

Any Demand?

Most teams never reach out for their help. Conversely, when certain teams reach out for help, there is nobody ready to deliver the benefit of coaching.

Time and Freedom

Whitespace time is agreeable to certain division leaders, but not others. We need all major business units (BUs) to have a "Time & Freedom" style program in place.

Culture of Innovation

As the Prizmic Labs team, reporting into the Office of CTO, we will be responsible for Prizmic's culture of innovation. We see culture as the manifestation of behaviors. Therefore we work to both define the behaviors we'd like to see, and to "be the change we wish to see."

To drive these improvements, we -

Define: We take the top CEO priorities and work in lockstep to help define actionable innovation mechanisms. Our employees can then use these mechanisms to achieve their goals. For example, Customer value models and Rapid Prototyping sessions helped the culture last fiscal year.

Vision Exercise - the <u>Future Press Release</u> for Prizmic Labs

Press Release

Prizmic Labs Innovation Center helps Prizmic Inc. doubles the growth rate of industry peers.

San Francisco--(BUSINESS WIRE)-- Aug. 1, 2015 -- (NASDAQ: PZMC) — Prizmic Inc. stunned Wall Street by delivering **double-digit growth for the fifth straight quarter**. Prizmic rocked the software and technology services sector, achieving double the growth rate of its nearest peer (Google). Gross margins also improved dramatically due to the successful shifts to high-scale service-based architectures. Prizmic also lowered costs to acquire customers and simultaneously improved customer retention rates, all while stealing market share from a multitude of former competitors and startups.

Prizmic's unique metric of **"increased primary value delivered to customers" showed a 12x improvement year over year**. Prizmic's growth rate and customer value improvement was accompanied by an unheard of **92%** Standardized Annual Employee Survey **(AES) employee engagement score** and **95% AES Innovation Practices score.** These factors launched Prizmic to the **#1 position** on the Forbes "Most Innovative Companies" list for the first time in their history.

At the root of this dramatic improvement in results was the 'Prizmic Labs' team. This team began their journey by helping teams focus on what matters most to customers. This laser-focus on value, in the customer's eyes, helped the entire company deliver to their customer benefit metrics. The Prizmic Labs team used their proprietary organizational change approaches to radically transform *what* product teams develop, and *how* product teams got their work done. Product team throughput was reportedly increased by 163% over the last 12 months. By building upon Prizmic's existing best practices, amplifying the methodologies which make an impact and dampening the ones which do not, the Prizmic Labs Team was able to overcome the challenges faced by most transformational change efforts.

The Labs team transformed Prizmic by:

- Re-focusing strategy on "customer benefits" as well as business metrics
- Leveraging core capabilities: Putting the customer needs center-stage, and using design thinking to solve those needs
- Encouraging project teams to consider "services-first" architectures, encouraging internal and external teams to deliver innovative Prizmic solutions
- Demanding Prizmic be more courageous, and bold, in the opportunities pursued

Bennett Chastain, Prizmic VP of Global Product Management comments: "After working with the Prizmic Labs Team, we quickly identified the benefits on which to focus. This gave us confidence to take bolder leaps. We started to develop more innovative ideas. For the first time, our team felt we were rapidly helping our customers."

Kim Niellson, Director of Corporate Product Infrastructure comments:"Frankly, I was skeptical this and the Labs approach would work. We explore new management initiatives each year, but none of them seem to make a lasting change. Based on pressure from our CEO, I explored this new way of working. And it worked! I've never felt more confident I'll be able to meet the expectations placed on me."

Resource: Prizmic Innovation Leader Job Description

Innovation Leader - Prizmic Innovation and Advanced Technology Group

Prizmic is seeking a highly-motivated, passionate leader to join our Innovation and Advanced Technology team. The Innovation leader will own the overall strategy and approach for driving increasing levels of innovation across Prizmic. The ideal candidate will be able to evaluate the performance of current programs and projects, develop new approaches for the company, and spin-up new programs that influence employees across the organization.

Responsibilities

The innovation leader will drive the strategic direction for improved innovation outcomes across the company.

Here is a small set of things you may do:
- Iterate the programs for customer research and product pilot programs
- Develop training materials to help product teams innovate for customers
- Build the most vibrant innovation culture in the industry
- Enable Prizmic to deliver increasingly valuable solutions to customers, year over year
- Connect senior leadership with our bottom-up innovation activity

This job is amazing because:
- You have autonomy: You own your projects. Working directly with your customers, the employees, you are self--directed and can see the change you are driving. We value your creativity, and you are using it every day to create a better future.
- You're part of a great team: We value autonomy, but we also value

small, agile, teams that drive great outcomes. Our employees are exceptional thinkers, motivated, and prioritize collaboration. We learn from each other, laugh, play, coach, kibbitz, and grow together each day. Life is more meaningful meaningful when you care for the people you work with on a daily basis.

- You're making an impact: Your self-authored goals and metrics make your progress clear, visible, and appreciated. You'll point to projects, products, and people and think, "I helped make that great thing happen."

We're looking for:

- A quick learner. The world's changing fast, are you changing faster?
- Passion for innovation. This is the subject, do you crave mastery?
- An evidence-based leader. Can you synthesize complex data into clear principles and smart decisions?
- A problem solver. Do you find a way to get to the finish line regardless of the challenge?
- A teambuilder. Our best teams amplify energy. Are you a 50 Kilowatt energy amplifier?

Experience

- Track records matter. The Innovation Leader will ideally have led killer new innovative initiatives from start to finish.
- A minimum 5-8+ years of related and progressive product development or product leadership experience is required.
- Experience with partnerships across organizational boundaries is essential.
- Working knowledge of intellectual property and patent strategies is highly desired for the role.
- An undergraduate degree in Engineering or Science is preferred and an advanced degree in engineering or management is desired.

Resource: "What's the Whitespace Times?" Newsletter

The Whitespace Times

Volume 4, Issue 6

Recent Results

This continues to be a banner year for Whitespace Time delivering new high-water marks in results and participation. 57 Whitespace Time initiatives were adopted so far by business units and functional groups across Prizmic (see the full list of successes on our <u>WhitespacePortal</u> linked to the corporate home menu).

Utilization

51% of employees surveyed said they used Whitespace Time. The result is "flat" compared with last month's 49% measurement of trailing 90-days usage of Whitespace TIme.

Wins

Congratulations to the Spark Sprint team (Abe Wickerton, Aaron Tripathi, Eve Delargy, and Hendro Battles) for their Edison Innovation Award and to "Leaning-Out : the marketing funnel optimizer" founders Ed Locketon and Ben Shiflett for winning the annual CEO Leadership Award. Once again, grassroots innovation is driving tangible results felt across the company.

We measured a big impact to Annual Employee Survey (AES) results this year. Higher business unit employee engagement was shown to correlate (at $r=0.76$) to higher Whitespace Time usage.
At the midpoint of this fiscal year, based on AES results, we were able

to correlate Whitespace Time usage to job satisfaction and innovation leadership scores. We found that users of Whitespace Time scored 13% higher in the "collaboration" category of AES engagement scores, and 9% higher in "excitement about business/offering strategy".

By the end of last month we'd added over 200 new Horizon 4s to the pipeline. (Horizon 4s, or H4s, are H3s that are not yet funded, read more on our portal). And the "Yo, You're Awesome" innovation contest from last quarter added another 170 projects in one month.

Some of the larger wins this year so far are: Online Projects Worldwide, Voice-it for Android, and Prizmic Military Edition. Not initially started this year, but shipping in a big way were Whitespace Time-originated projects Prizmic-Life Online for iPad), Prizmic on wheels and Jump for Joy Mobile. Kudos to these teams!

A Hack Day is the Way!

Have you ever felt frustrated trying to find the time or support to turn your idea into a product you can test with real customers? Or perhaps you even have made great progress during Whitespace Time and just need that final boost of testing with customers to reach the next level.

At Prizmic, we have an on-going set of Hack Days plus special "on-demand Hacks" that our Whitespace Time core team can help with. Sign up here. If you haven't used Whitespace Time in a while, realize you've saved up time to work on your idea. But even better, Whitespace Time enthusiasts are on hand to provide whatever help your team needs to make progress. We'll help you gain customer empathy, design, build experiments, learn from customers, and create the next big Prizmic winner!

Highlights of the Month

The last Enterprise Group Hack Day was rocking and rolling fast. As one example, after 1 and a half days of effort, the Prizmic "Recipes for Success" team sat down and talked with us about their early journey. They felt that after some quick adjustments they found the path for learning about what delights their customers.

Innovators: sign-up for a Hack Day and accelerate your project! We're now accepting enthusiastic applicants.

Upcoming Events

Boston-based Innovation guru Scott Karunthers is coming to town on October 21st with his "Innovation Leader Field Study." Come by to hear from his 55 senior innovation execs from companies like The Gap, Nike, Medtronic, Procter & Gamble, Disney and Thomson Reuters. Let's learn about their methodologies as they learn from us during a 60 minute immersive session! Sign up.

Helping Give Back with Nonprofits and Non-Governmental Groups

Our Prizmic "Care and Give" program welcomes all innovators to drop by the skills-giving maker space in building 2 Menlo Park each Thursday afternoon to help ongoing projects for social good. Join a team, accept a challenge, or just grab a short-term weekly task to help our partner organizations help people in need.

And above all, remember to use Whitespace Time and to apply for Intrapreneurship Week.

Resource: Intrapreneurship Week Resources

The Intrapreneurship Week resources help capture the materials and guidelines needed to run a great Intrapreneurship Week.

This resource pack includes:

- Overview of Intrapreneurship Week
- Agenda
- Designing your MVP
- Following up after Intrapreneurship Week

Overview - Intrapreneurship Week

The mission of our Prizmic LABS incubator is to accelerate Prizmic's journey to becoming an amazing innovation company by increasing the yield of successful new businesses from our grassroots innovation. Intrapreneurship Week is here to help us live this mission and reach our goal of increasing the yield of successful new businesses from our grassroots innovation.

Each Intrapreneurship week is captured as a pipeline of innovation ideas (see the pipeline collection in BrightIdea)

At Intrapreneurship Week you work with the Prizmic Labs Team and your peers to:

- Transform visions Into reality

- Push forward to build your MVP

- Have your passion amplified!

- Get real help from real innovation coaches (beyond lectures)

Intrapreneurship week runs for all 5 days, with teams starting at 9AM each morning in the Innovation Design area. The selected incubative teams often make a month's worth progress in a week.

We've recently kicked off this focus on intrapreneurship here at Prizmic by forming the new Prizmic LABS Incubator.

Monthly, we're accepting a total of 5 teams into a week-long incubation session.

Quickly make progress with your product-market fit and rapid experimentation with customers.

Teams that are accepted can quickly make progress by building the Minimum Viable Product (MVP) that helps them learn what most needs to be learned, from customer behavior. If accepted to this first Intrapreneurship Week, you'll receive:

- a cool t-shirt,
- food and drinks,
- resources to help you build!
- access to customers,
- design resources (on-site incubator designer ready to help)
- broad Prizmic exposure, and
- mentorship from special guests.

Agenda for the week

Monday

- 9:00 AM Overview of the week, *Patty*
- 9:10 AM Overview of Prizmic LABS Intrapreneurship, *Carol*
- 9:20 AM Tools we will use during the week, *Boris*
- 9:30 AM Teams work on their Business Model Canvases

Tuesday

- 9:00 AM Check in

- 9:10 AM Ice breaker - Group improv, 'I am a tree" or 'proverbs' to warm up
- 9:30 AM - 5:00 PM Unblocking, mentoring, specify your experiment loop and build the MVP you need to learn what you need to learn

Wednesday

- 9:00 AM Check in
- 9:10 AM Ice breaker - Group improv, 'I am a tree" or 'proverbs' to warm up
- 9:30 AM - 5:00 PM Unblocking, mentoring, specify your experiment loop and build the MVP you need to learn what you need to learn

Thursday

- 9:00 AM Check in
- 9:30 AM Teams work on their experiment loop charts, rapid experimentation, etc.
- 2:00 PM As needed, teams check in with legal launch team to get immediate eeprt help on branding, privacy, etc. as needed
- 3:30 PM Attend site social for food, drinks, conversation

Friday

- 9:00 AM - Check in
- 9:15 AM Video interviews, team one by one go to describe their week and their MVP
- 11:30 AM Check on Gallery Walk readiness
- 2:30 PM – 3:30 PM Gallery Walk, show your stuff!

Notes - (fold in other Key portions of the agenda, ice-breakers, peer huddles)

About the Friday Gallery Walk

This is team's opportunity to show the MVPs built, to talk about the innovation, to go deep with the interested employees who come by. We will also have a number of execs and special guests coming by.

1. Show the Vision and Design Principles Tool

2. Show your Lean Experimentation map

3. Be able to tell the crisp "elevator pitch" story of your week

Designing Your MVP

Designing effective experiments is one of the most important skills to master as a Lean Startup practitioner. The results from your experiments should be credible enough to make decisions, based on the data and insights created during the experiment. In order to have confidence in the data and insights, keep the following principles in mind.

Always measure real customer behavior!

- Focus on behaviors that your customers *must* do for your idea to work
- Experiment only on your target customers
- Set aggressive metrics (numbers that will get you excited!)
- **Go FAST** – *run your experiment quickly!*
- **Pro Tip:** *Work hard to remain unbiased. Design your experiment so that even a "skeptic" can re-run your experiment and get the same results.*

Popular Types of MVPs for Rapid Experimentation:

- **Concierge MVP (Holy Grail)**: Manually perform tasks which will eventually be automated, even if you lose money initially.
- **Fake-O App**: Present an App as if it was live, with only simple home page and sign-up flows. This website should feel real, and capture currency.
- **Judo (Imposter)**: Use a competitor or related website/product to gather data, as if it were your own website/product. Repackage an existing product.
- **Analog/Retro**: Sell a physical version of the product, even if your final product will be digital.
- **Dry-Wallet**: Experiments which present a fake purchase experience, in order to test a business model or strong market signal from consumer.

- **Human IVR:** A person acts like an Integrated Voice Response system, but records customer choices, adapts the flow to learn more, and works a customer interview into the end of the call.

Additional Experiment Ideas: These experiments are often used in conjunction with the experiments listed above. Mix and match for your situation.

- **Letters of Intent:** Non-binding commitment to purchase your solution in the future (good for B2B concepts)
    - Currency: Willingness to commit to LOI, sign name
- **Storyboards:** Visual story of the problem your product is solving
    - Currency: Feedback and emotional response to your idea.
- **Mock-Ups:** Static mock-ups for a product which does not yet exist.
    - Currency: Feedback and emotional response to your idea.
- **Video Trailers:** Video trailer of a product (hint: use with Fake-O)
    - Currency: Feedback and emotional response to your idea.

Develop a business model which fits the preferred model for your customer. "Charge" your customer in a manner in which your customer prefers. Keep in mind we're using the word "charge" in the abstract, since your business model may involve "free" offerings where the customer does not pay for your product (but we extract economic value in some other way.

- **Unit Sales** - Sell a product or service to customers for a fee. Often employs multi-tier product lineups. Examples: Nike shoes, TurboTax, QuickBooks
- **Advertising** - Sell opportunities to distribute messages to end users, or lead generation. Examples: The New York Times, network television, blogs, Mint.com
- **Transaction** - Charge a fee referring, enabling, or executing a transaction between multiple parties. Examples: Visa, eBay, see IPN and Prizmic Payments
- **Utilization** - Sell goods and services on a per-use or as-consumed basis. Examples: Utilities, mobile phone minutes, GB storage, Prizmic

banking services

- **Subscription** - Charge a fixed price for access to your services for a period of time or series of uses. Examples: 24-Hour fitness, QuickBooks Online, etc.

- **Franchise** - Sell and support a replicable business for others to invest in, grow, and manage locally. Examples: McDonald's, etc.

- **Professional** - Provide professional services on a time–and-materials contract. Examples: Consultants, architects, designers, QB Certified Accountants, etc.

- **License** - Sell the rights to use intellectual property. Examples: NFL Team logos, patents, some software, see Quicken Loans.

- **Pay-per-performance** – Customer pays only when desired outcome is achieved, typically based on value of the outcome. Examples: AdWords, affiliate commissions, GE service uptime guarantee,

- **Internal Business Models** – For internal Prizmic innovations, "currency" and value may be measured in cost reduction, time savings, other business metrics, etc. Examples: Call reduction, time to market, up-sells, sales optimization, etc.

Measurement in your MVP

MixPanel is a web analytics platform. Everything on MixPanel is based on engagement actions users take in your application (web or mobile). MixPanel doesn't track page views by default because actions, and metrics associated with actions, are generally more useful for understanding your users' behavior. An action can be as simple as a tweet, purchase, video play, or signup.

You can easily use the MixPanel account that the Prizmic Labs Incubator team has already set for you. Please see your coach.

Following up: After the End of Intrapreneurship Week

Teams will have monthly check-ins, be prepared to discuss the following:

- Experiments run to date

- What was measured

- What was learned

- What's next (next leap of faith hypothesis)

Assessing Progress

Unit of one "Love Metrics"

- Deliver the customer benefit
- Customer actively uses
- Customer willing to recommend (NPS)
- Frame a hypothesis for who will pay for the offering

"Love Metrics" Questions:
1. What is your customer benefit?
2. How do you measure your customer benefit?
3. How do you truly understand the benefit your app is delivering?
4. What is the 1 Key metric that explains your hypothesis, and what are you doing to get this?
5. How can you build NPS into every app?
6. Do you understand why your promoters are promoters and why your detractors are detractors?
7. What is your biggest surprise?

Email template

To help spread the news and get more innovations out there, please use this template to invite your colleagues to Intrapreneurship Week.

WHO: We want YOU for Intrapreneurship Week!

WHAT: Intrapreneurship Week is a great way to keep moving with your project and ideas. You'll receive resources to help you build, access to customers, design resources, broad Prizmic exposure, and mentorship from special guests.

WHY: If accepted, you can quickly make progress by building the Minimum Viable Product (MVP) that helps you learn what you most need to learn (from customer behavior, peers, etc).

WHEN: We're holding this next Intrapreneurship Week [MONTH][DAY1]-DAY5].

HOW: To apply, please email IntrapreneurshipWeek@Prizmic.com

Design Thinking Key Resources

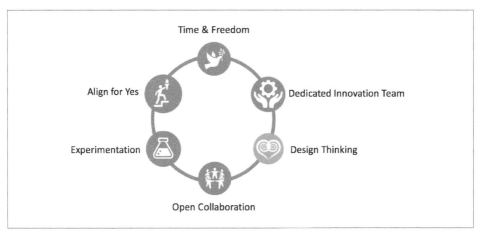

Resource: Designing Joy (Design Thinking Workshop)

From: Carol Jacobs
To: Whitespace_Time_Taskforce
Subject: Let's do this thing! Design Thinking at Prizmic

Patty and team,

I'm so excited about this I can barely contain myself. So hopefully you'll excuse my over the top enthusiasm, and excessive use of exclamation points! But this is an awesome opportunity! :-)

Here's the deal: We <u>must </u>launch and propagate a Design Thinking program across the company. The opportunity is too great to pass up. The downside is too awful to consider. My reasoning is this: Design Thinking gives us principles and structure for how to put the customer at the center of everything we do. Sure, we want engineers playing with technology and maybe even doing things that aren't focused on a customer need. But, at the end of the day, all our efforts must be channeled towards making life better for our customer. Otherwise our efforts actions, words, and even deeds, don't amount to actually moving the needle for customers.

The essence of what I learned at Stanford D. School is this (that's Stanford's 'design school' by the way! :-)):

1) Design Thinking is all about principles that get us better results for customers
2) It is a teachable skillset
3) It is reasonable, and desirable, to try to teach the basics of Design Thinking to everyone. I mean every single person in the company!
4) For the people with special passion and appetite for all this, we can teach them more and more to the point they become great at Design Thinking. This gives us our crop of training, the coaches for coaches, an ever growing bunch of expert trainers.

I propose we start with agreeing on the principles. Then we can look over and hopefully commit to starting with a one day immersive training for the people most anxious to learn about Design Thinking. Please read over the rest of this note and send your feedback!

- Your 'Care Bear' Carol

Key points: Our Brand of Design Thinking

Design thinking, in its essence, is a set of mindsets and tools that emphasize three thing: A focus on deep customer empathy, exploring a multitude of possibilities (going broad) before narrowing down to decision points and employing rapid experimentation with customers.

Deep Customer Empathy

To achieve deep customer empathy, we attempt to understand the customer better than they understand themselves. This requires the discipline to set aside our own opinions and observe customers performing tasks in their own natural environments. To fully uncover a customer's motivations, we not only capture what they do and say, we also want to try to capture what they are thinking and feeling.

Going Broad Before Narrowing

In human nature, when faced with a problem, we tend to fall in love with the very first solution that comes to mind. Studies have shown that it's very unlikely that the first solution that occurs to us will be the best solution and it's best to go for quantity of ideas first (Osborn, A.F. (1963) Applied imagination: Principles and procedures of creative problem solving (Third Revised Edition). New York, NY: Charles Scribner's Sons). Going Broad To Go Narrow imposes the discipline of creating options before making choices. Often the best idea will surface after dozens of other ideas or it may be an amalgamation of several ideas.

Rapid Experimentation

Rather than attempting to implement a perfect plan in a waterfall approach, Design Thinking dictates that you accept that your ideas will be fundamentally flawed at the start and that getting to a delightful product requires rapid experiments with customers and learning how to make the product better.

Training our Employees

Let's roll this out like the training at D School. What if we call it "Designing Joy"? DJ for short. Our DJ program may be cool (and gives us an excuse to kick off each day playing tunes!)

And let's use an Immersive teaching formula. That means, instead of lecturing, each segment follows the flow: Describe it, show it, each person does it, give and get feedback, then do it again.

For example, on the customer empathy training we can describe what it is, have people practice observing and deriving empathy, write it down, get feedback on the findings. And we'll pull in best available materials. For example, on empathy the D.School site has materials, empathy maps, (at d.school stanford site, in the "use our methods" section).

Agenda for Day - Designing Joy, 'DJ' Overview Session (shallow immersion)

- 9:00 AM - 10:00 AM **What is empathy?**
  - Watch Brene Brown TED Talk on empathy, that is learning empathy!
  - Discuss Dr. Brown's view of empathy
- 10:15AM - 11:30 AM **Customer interviews**
  - Go over the essence of a great probing interview, design question guide
  - Bring in customers, interview
  - Report back surprises and observations to the room
- 11:30AM - 12:05 PM **Empathy maps**

- Lunch
- 1:00 - 1:45 PM **Problem statements**
- 1:45 - 2:15 PM **Brainstorm solutions**
- 2:30 - 3:15 PM **Build Rapid Prototype**s
- 3:30 - 4:15 PM **Test with customers**
- 4:15 - 4:45 PM **Report findings back to the room**
- 4:45 - 5:00 PM **Reflection on the day**
  - + - deltas, Net Promoter Feedback Survey completed

Resource: Making the Case for Design Thinking

Anyone can be a successful intrapreneur. To successfully create a culture where everyone innovates, you must equip your employees with Design Thinking skills. Then every employee, whether they work in HR, IT, Product, Legal or Finance, can be an intrapreneur.

This is because Design Thinking helps your intrapreneurs to focus on developing innovative solutions that match customer needs. Design Thinking guides both the "what will constitute a good target for innovation, as well as the "how to effectively innovate". Without Design Thinking human nature tends to take over, and us humans dive straight into our own opinions, and quickly fall in love with our own opinions and solutions. Sometimes this works, but for the most part, the highly opinionated, solution-back thought process generates lots of expensive solutions to problems that may not even truly exist.

Design Thinking was born of pattern recognition. What works, what has happened when we see people achieve great innovative results? When observing how people innovate most effectively, a few consistently recurring patterns emerge. Getting close to customers, understanding what they truly care about and need, is fundamental. Then, we often see that the most effective results come from deeply understanding the customer's needs while broadly exploring a multitude of approaches. Prematurely locking into a "solution we love" has been the downfall of many a new hopeful service, app, or company. Rather, the people and teams that think big and broad, experiment with a number of approaches, often then find their way to a winning solution. And that success path often represent at least four or five "unforeseen" curves it the road.

Fortunately, a set of principles and framework that "collects" these patterns into a neat package already exists. It is called Design Thinking.

When companies figure out how to infuse their culture with Design

Thinking, employees focus on customer needs, innovate with speed and a precise attention to learning from customers as they go, and therefore drive better business results. A multitude of companies have taken the plunge, switching over from a more tops down large, big-bet strategic innovative focus to a more "process oriented" focus on Design Thinking principles. And by process oriented we means the processes related to deep customer learning, prototyping, iterative testing, and the more entrepreneurial mechanism for finding the path to customer delight. Companies like Apple, Google, P&G, IBM, Samsung, SAP, Nordstrom, Citrix, and so many others, are enthusiastic advocates of Design Thinking. Infusing your company culture with Design Thinking can start as simply as empowering a few advocates and setting up an introductory training course, or can be a deeper commitment we see at companies that hire and train dozens of not hundreds of skilled design thinkers to work within teams across the entire organization

Defining Design Thinking

Design Thinking outlines the key principles and methods for successful intrapreneurship. To be effective, your Intrapreneurs must develop true customer empathy, quickly build prototypes, build a bit more of the solution, run experiments, iterate, and thereby change the world. But these things don't happen accidentally. The process, the know-how to develop solutions that customer actually want to use, is a skillset. And not a particularly intuitive skill-set at that. Few people are born able to immediately absorb the principles of Design Thinking.

To be a great design thinker, you must suppress human nature, particularly the tendency to love our own solutions. It's hard to not love your own ideas, everybody gets that. But what turns out to be much more valuable is an intense focus on the problem to be solved. The self-discipline to stay rooted in the problem space, rather than quickly jumping to our own ideas about creative solutions, is a wonderful virtue. As Albert Einstein said, "It's not that I'm so smart, it's just that I stay with problems longer. If I had an hour to solve a problem, I'd spend 55 minutes thinking about the problem and 5 minutes thinking about solutions."

Einstein knew the hardest, but most valuable step in creative problem solving, is to deeply consider the problem to solve as well as the root cause of this problem. And after that, talented design thinkers explore lots of possible solutions, not just the first exciting solution that comes to mind.

But possibly the most powerful aspect of Design Thinking is the notion of developing deep empathy for the customer. Finding customer empathy, and keeping the resultant insights and "Ahas" as the center of focus are core tenants of Design Thinking.

The Business Case for Design Thinking

Design Thinking makes great business sense. For example, startup company AirBnB had run into a fundamental roadblock: People didn't want to rent places to stay from them. In exploring why, the previously engineering hyperfocused founders realized they could talk to would be customers and get a sense of why the places offered weren't renting. THis "empathy gathering" approached returned a clear result. Common discussion themes were "why would I want to stay there?" The underlying root cause seemed to be the places to stay looked like crap. Not the deepest customer empathy ever discovered, to be sure, this issue of "I want to stay somewhere more appealing" was a strong signal.

The AirBnb folks then embarked on a photography field trip, working to test the hypothesis of "maybe if we have beautiful hi resolution images of each property, people will want to actually stay at these places." Thus rapid experimentation, with nothing more than a few cameras, existing web technology and a few plane tickets, enabled the team to test and learn.

The AirBnb replaced low res, poorly considered property photos with nice hi resolution photos.Results were fast. Revenues doubled within a week.

This quick and successful Design Thinking experiment changed things at Airbnb forever. The company shifted from a focus on code to getting outside the building to meet with customers and dig into what they think, feel and truly need. Airbnb cloned this Design Thinking mantra to other parts of the company, including new employee onboarding. Airbnb employees leave the building and take a trip within two weeks of joining. The new employees learn about customers by observing and documenting what customers do.

The these new employees share back their experiences to other employees. After the customer field trip, every employee is encouraged to come up with and share their innovative ideas.

When you teach your employees to absorb the principles of Design Thinking and see the world through this very special lens, three primary business benefits come to life:

1. Laser focus on customer needs. Correctly identifying customer needs increases significantly in companies that teach employees DT skills. Whether the customer is internal - for example the recipient of Human Resources help -- or external end-user customers who purchase a service or product, DT's tools and mindsets for identifying problems and opportunities set the stage for deeply understanding customers and what they need.

2. Fast and lean execution. As teams gain fast results coming from proven or disproven hypotheses, these teams often garner quick wins and fast fails. And those fast fails are of course wins as well. Because Design Thinking emphasizes rapid experimentation with customers, teams can avoid the most hurtful time-waster of all - designing and building stuff nobody wants.

3. Increased Growth and Profitability. Companies that train their employees in Design Thinking transform behavior in a wonderful way, including an increased focus on what customers truly care about. A nice "byproduct" of this transformation is that both top and bottom lines improve when each employee develops DT skills.

Companies that have become known for utilizing Design Thinking -- P&G, SAP, Apple, Intuit, IBM, IDEO, Airbnb, Intuit, Infosys, Pinterest, Fidelity, Toshiba, and so many others -- have flourished. And the multitude of companies that either lost their way, or never tried the DT approach, have been more challenged. Without the focus on customer needs, the use of broad and generative thinking combined with a strong capability to prioritize well and focus, companies waste time and money. And the companie that have eschewed testing, learning fast, finding new workable paths, just aren't suited to beat their more agile, fast-learning competitors.[1]

---

[1] http://digitalsurgeons.com/thoughts/design-thinking/5-big-organizations-that-win-with-design-thinking

The Arguments Against

I don't see Design Thinking as scientifically proven. Where are all the longitudinal studies showing Design Thinking as the answer?

Control group experiments are difficult here: Who wants to be the company or team that doesn't use Design Thinking, as the competition handedly annihilates you? That said, research from the Hasso Plattner design institute is fairly conclusive[1], but in an inductive reasoning sense. When analyzing the things that lead to making your employees effective innovations, the act of "building those innovators", DT registers as the "how". How people work to generate creative solutions to difficult problems, is the inductive lens that has generated DT.

So Design Thinking comes empirically observing, studying, developing patterns and brader concepts of how to work.
As one example of success using Design Thinking principles, Procter and Gamble's adopted Design Thinking and saw one of their strong brands, Tide[2], increase revenue from $12 billion to almost $24 billion. The brand is now surging in emerging markets.

Design Thinking slows everything down, so why slow our company down?

It may be true the fastest thing possible, according to the clock and calendar, is to quickly build whatever you'd like to. This can be a fast endeavor. However, the solutions built using this "just run with my opinion, build it all out, and ship it" tend to miss the mark and not accomplish anything. So if we define speed as velocity towards impactful results that actually achieve the target results, then achieving speed becomes a whole new endeavour. Design Thinking keeps us focused on getting to the customer's need, solving the right thing at the right time, while iteratively testing our way to the result. This is the way to get the actually desired results in the fastest manner possible. For example, Intuit brought 32 new innovations to market quickly after inspiring employees to use Design Thinking principles to gather empathy and learn quickly from customers.

---

[1] http://springer.com/us/book/9783319068220
[2] http://hbr.org/2011/06/how-pg-tripled-its-innovation-success-rate

Design is great, but pretty doesn't win, awesome technology wins, right?

It's not about pretty, it's about meeting the true needs of customers (empathy) with just the right solutions (rapid experimentation). Conversely, the most brilliant and snazzy technological innovation, used in the wrong way and the wrong time, achieves absolutely nothing positive for customers.

Design Thinking creates a cult of the powerful and obsessive great designers, taking too ouch power away from the executives who need to lead the strategic thinking

Mauro Porcini, PepsiCo's first-ever chief design officer, said he was hired to spread design thinking at the 118-year-old company. He found "endless examples" of projects that the business team had rejected. To help colleagues shift to saying yes from no, his team began to produces prototypes of new ideas before debating the pros and cons.
When Porcini's team conceptualized an emoji campaign for the Pepsi bottle, for example, company execs were already working with an external agency. "So they went on their own way, and we kept prototyping, we kept presenting." Eventually, prototypes helped Porcini's team's ideas win colleagues over[1].

Design Thinking seems to shut out business model innovation, which often is the most important innovation for companies! So knock it off with all the Design Thinking pushing.

"Whether you are interested in business model innovation or not you should be leveraging design thinking and process to improve your customer experience. It is a requirement for business model innovation. In fact, maybe we need to bang together the heads of mad scientists and mad designers. If we are waiting for lengthy business plans with detailed financial analysis and randomized double blind studies to tell us if a new business model is viable we will be waiting a very long time. That is not how business model innovation works. It takes passionate exploration, which is more iterative than traditional scientific methodology. It takes design thinking and process

---

[1] http://fortune.com/2017/03/14/singapore-design-week-business

combined with powerful storytelling to create novel business models. We need to try more stuff and design thinking and process can help."[1]

Companies That Are Good Examples

Hundreds if not thousands of cases of Design Thinking successes are out there[2]. And it is the intrinsically motivated Intrapreneurs, in control of their own time, focused on bold challenges, that make the best use of Design Thinking. You need to put employees in control of their schedules, help them carve out time for intrapreneurship, and then help them use Design Thinking during the time they have for intrapreneurship.

Chris Carter was CEO of the startup QuitNet.com (aimed at helping people quit smoking), and then became head of **MeYou Health**, the Internet strategy division of healthcare services giant Healthways. He used design thinking techniques like journaling to understand consumer health attitudes and practices, and personas to map out different behavioural clusters, eg. idle, excuse makers, validation seekers, enlightened and 'me-time impoverished.' Prototyping on MVPs via social media eventually led to the Daily Challenge, a gamified approach to help people with their health-improving actions.

3M used 'design provocation' to transform its B2B sales process.[3] Ethnographic research was used to better understand potential customers in the context of sales pitches, and 'future use-case' videos, photographs and stories were used to excite and inspire customers. Finding internal change champions helped create new kinds of formal and informal conversations via quantitative and qualitative tools.

Entrepreneurship champions Jean Byrne and Jim Dunne, co-founders of consultancy firm Design21C, helped the city of **Dublin** move away from its bureaucratic approach and engage citizens more actively to rebuild the city. The World Cafe approach, along with numerous surveys, helped pick three clusters for change: water, waste and community. Nine potential projects for urban renewal were shortlisted and described via online and cardboard models in public spaces. A spirit of fun, citizen engagement and self-selection helped win broad support across the board.

---

1. http://fortune.com/2012/05/02/the-problem-with-design-thinking
2. http://goodreads.com/book/show/17938813-solving-problems-with-design-thinking
3. http://yourstory.com/2015/05/problem-solving-with-design-thinking

Experience marketing firm George P. Johnson helped **IBM** transform its trade show experience for customers from spectacles into conversations, from monologue to dialogue. This was achieved by a combination of seating and standing areas, public and private spaces, and formal and informal settings to accommodate different learning styles of audiences. Card games were used as internal learning tools, and the focus shifted from just quantitative 'badge' metrics to 'behavioural metrics' of client engagement based on learning models. Ethnographic research was used to study customers as well as IBM employees at trade show booths.

Amazon, **Zappos** and **Easyjet** are companies that have done a good job of identifying and redefining value; **Pixar University** reinforces a creative culture[1] through a range of courses.

At **AirBnB** - they keep the details secret - but conceptually AirBnB committed to Design Thinking, to deeply understanding the needs of their users (both renters and rentees). The AirBnB user base is quite diverse. Sometimes the situation arises that a request does not match the host's lifestyle or expectations of what a »proper guest« may look and behave like (just think of young Berlin party tourists trying to book the quiet apartment of an elderly couple). In such or similar occasions the likelihood of hosts rejecting or not responding is relatively high. Even though one might feel sympathetic to the host's decision, the user experience for the guest breaks. Especially inexperienced first time users are unlikely to come back. AirBnB knows exactly, that running a multi-sided platform model entails the mediation and facilitation of user relations. It therefore has to find ways to resolve or prevent such conflicts, e.g. by adequately matching certain user profiles. In order to do that however it first had to know *why hosts reject*, i.e. what are reasons that aren't understood yet and how may they be addressed?

---

[1] http://yourstory.com/2014/01/book-review-design-thinking-strategic-innovation/

Case Study: Intuit's Innovation Catalysts

Intuit's journey into the domain of Design Thinking can easily be seen as a "hero's journey," addressing a challenging call to action[1].
 Here's what happened at Intuit, and why:

Act I

1. **Realization**: Intuit co-founder Scott Cook realizes the company has lost it's way; solving big unmet customers needs has lost its traction. Net Promoter Scores had been falling. Progress is too incremental, too mediocre, not customer-led.

2. **Insight**: Scott feels he is not Steve Jobs, he is not that mythically inventive leader from whom all breakthrough ideas for a company must emanate. There must be a different way.

3. **External inspiration**: Scott discussed his concern with Claudia Kotchka, then P&G's vice president of design innovation and strategy. He comes away with the notion that "Design Thinking" rather than just "great design" may be the answer.

Act II

4. **Take action, start small:** Scott discussed the opportunity with then CEO Steve Bennett. The decide to focus the company's top 300 managers on the role of design in innovation at an offsite. The one-day program would teach what was called "Design for Delight" (D4D), Intuit's flavor of Design Thinking. The event was meant to relaunch Intuit as a design-driven company.

5. **Fail, then try again:** Scott led the leaders through a PowerPoint presentation laying out the values of Design Thinking. People listened and applauded. The energy in the room was questionable, and then after the off-site — and the large investment of leadership time and effort — nothing seemed to happen

---

[1] http://hbr.org/2011/06/the-innovation-catalysts

6. **Immerse to engage:** Back to the drawing board. Scott hypothesized that the concepts needed to be more effectively taught. He met Alex Kazaks, a consulting professor and Stanford. Kazaks was brought in to present to employees in a 2-hour session. Kazakh uses a minimum pop Powerpoint and engaged the attendees in an immersive exercise. Attendees worked through a design challenge called "the wallet exercise". They gathered empathy, prototyped, iterated, and refined an innovation in real-time. The attendees were excited, as if seeing the value of a design-oriented process for the first time.

Act III

7. **Make it work:** With the formula for employee engagement in place (immersive training), and the principles of D4D solid and teachable, Intuit built a small central design team to spread the goodness. A first cadre of Innovation Catalysts (ICs), trained in D4D and committed to spending a minimum of 2 hours a month helping teams use D4D, was formed.

8. **Make it drive transformation:** The ICs evangelized the use of Jams (Pain jams for getting to customer pains and needs, and "Sol" Jams" -- short for solution Jams -- to get possible solutions ready for experimentation. As various divisions used the Design for Delight principles, with the help of ICs, more and more success stories were developed and retold. The success stories and measurable outcomes from new innovations with higher Net Promoter Scores and improved user engagement, cemented D4D as a visible part of the Intuit culture.

9. **Make it scale:** ICs became trainers and coaches of other ICs. The internal mentorship rule meant that each new IC had a more senior mentor to lean on. Careful attention was paid to coverage of ICs across each functional and business unit. This distribution resulted in nearly every function and business unit putting innovation points on the board. For example, the Finance division recently used rapid experimentation to fix and internal process which made customer communication more effective, resulting in a large bump in revenue

retention. The consumer products division invented a new mobile platform for tax filers who prefer to use their phone for nearly everything (resulting in the highest Net Promoter Score Intuit had ever received).

Experimentation Key Resources

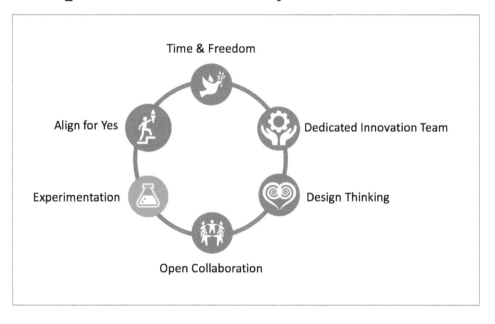

Resource: Lean Startup Worksheet

Lean Startup Worksheet   Product Name _____

1. Vision – *how will your product improve customers lives?*	2. Product Idea – *how will you accomplish your vision?*

3. Assumptions

#	Assumption – *what do you believe that must be true for your idea to succeed?*	Leap of Faith?

Check as "leap-of-faith" (LOFA) your riskiest assumptions:
1. The most important to be true
2. The least proven to be true

4. Experiments

LOFA #	Hypothesis – *Declare expected outcome:* [Specific Repeatable Action] will [Expected Measurable Outcome]	Minimum Viable Product – *describe the experiment vehicle you'll use to test your hypothesis*	Results – *what data did you collect?*	Learning – *validated or invalidated? Surprises?*

Align to Yes Key Resources

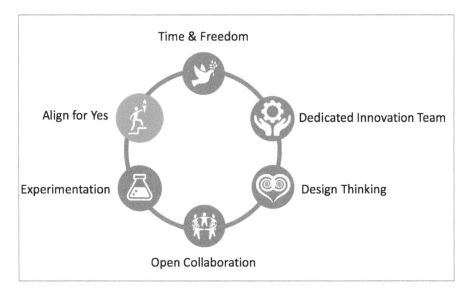

Template - Prizmic Horizon Model

	Horizon 1	Horizon 2	Horizon 3	Horizon 4
Purpose	Extend and defend core products	Build emerging products	Create viable options	Employee-generated ideas
Primary Activities	Optimization and Profitability (Innovating in the core)	Introduction and Scale (Investing in growth, learning how to scale)	In-market Experimentation (Delivering value proposition and business model hypothesis)	Discovery and Ideation (Discovering unsolved, important customer problem with compelling solution)
Graduation Criteria	N/A	Validated sustainable growth model (Scaled, profitable business)	Validated Product-Market Fit (Good market with product that can satisfy that market)	Validated "Love Metrics" (Delivered customer benefit, with customers actively using and positive word-of-mouth)
Team Type	"Rowing crew" (Large, coordinated functional teams)	"White water rafting" (Medium-sized team with functional specialists)	"Diving for sunken treasure" (Small teams with entrepreneurs wearing multiple hats)	
Typical Product Team Size	> 50	15 to 50	5 to 15	1 to 5

Template: How to Be a Better Coach

From: Carol Jacobs
To: Whitespace_Time_Taskforce
Subject: PLEASE REVIEW: Coaching across Prizmic

Team,

Patty, Boris and I had a great conversation about the importance of coaching. As we roll out our innovation programs., it will be important to remember we need to train up people to spread the innovation lessons and "make them stick". So we need to actually "coach the coaches" to skillfully provide expertise and guidance to our innovators.

Please review the coaching points and resources below.

Thanks!

Our company needs to double down on training-up more and more effective coaches.

We can look to certain exemplars to channel their world class coaching.

For example, Bill "Coach" Campbell was one of the most central and important contributors to Silicon Valley. Bill was a coach, leader, CEO, Board member at Google, Apple, Amazon, Intuit, and close friend to many. For Bill, coaching was all about trust and relationship.

Steve Jobs is another inspiration for our innovation coaching curriculum. Steve built the highest valued company in history. He understood that smart, effective, inspired employees would do amazing things. For Steve, coaching was about giant vision, beauty, customer value, and the desire to put a dent in the universe.

Scott Cook is another inspiration. Scott, co-founder of Intuit and know as the originator of Follow me Home customer studies, software usability testing, and customer-driven product innovation, has also mentored scores of top-notch corporate executives. For Scott, coaching is about amplifying employee's energy and helping people focus on the critical few priorities.

Our coaching curriculum should be a synthesis of the top coaching lessons from the Campbell, Cook, Jobs and some fo the other brilliant coaches we've encountered.

Here are the 26 key coaching points I propose form a basis for the pilot coaching course -

Concept	Key thoughts
Be a human	1. **Recognize what you see that you like**. Pure criticism is plain ineffective. Every person and team must be doing something good! Get excited about this thing you like, point it out. Then you have "one positive" as an anchor as you venture into more difficult territory. 2. **Hugs all around**. The underlying principle here leverages essential human nature. The coach who cares, who is real, and who is emotional, is the coach who will forge the deepest connection and earn the most respect. 3. **Avoid spilt milk discussion**. A wasteful thing to do is say "Oh, I wish you hadn't done this, it was wrong." Well that is 'spilt milk'. You can't rewind the clock to travel back in time. But what's helpful is to talk about what to now do moving forward.

Be focused and simplify	4. **Help them simplify**. Great coaches help people get to the clear and simple heart of the matter. As Steve Jobs said, "Simple can be harder than complex: You have to work hard to get your thinking clean to make it simple. But it's worth it in the end because once you get there, you can move mountains."
	5. **Emphasize** "it is better to hit a homerun than two doubles." Jobs would often coach this concept. Years back, in his blunt and painful style, Jobs told Nike's new CEO: "Get rid of the crappy stuff."
	6. **Teach prioritization**. Help people become brutal "list slashers." If they think 10 things are important, insist they pick the top two. Now, does the calendar match the priorities? Most people, when asked to see how they spend their time relative to those top priorities, see that life is out of whack. Great coaches make it clear this lack of prioritization must stop.
	7. **Get the key issue out on the table.** Get people to express their challenge, their dilemma or debate. Instead of leading with your own ideas, ask people to describe what help they want to receive. And if you give them help where they want the help they will be more likely come back for more
	8. **Think about "what is the thing I want them to do?"** Can they do it on their own? Or after the person or teams describe their big issue, instead of solving it for them, work on the problem together.
	9. **Help with criteria.** Often a team will have trouble defocusing and narrowing because they disagree on the criteria. So do it together. Have them list the possible criteria and then narrow.
	10. **Find the one thing.** As a coach, diagnose the "what's the one thing this team/person most needs?" Often it takes a concerted effort, observing beneath surface level, to reach this conclusion.

Be a Storyteller	11. **Tell short, relevant stories**. These short stories will become your primary teaching mechanism. Droll "Bueller, Bueller" soliloquies don't work, in fact they are painful for all. Skip the lecturing and engage others with your short "key lesson" stories.
Cultivate energy	12. **Leave them energized**. If the team leaves energized, great things can happen. If the team leaves demoralized, even if the coaching seemed great, nothing good will happen. How to leave them energized and feeling excited about their mission? That's easy if the team is just in need of cheerleading. But, it's not so easy if rougher topics of discussion come up. Tie back to what is positive, what you liked, by the end.
	13. **Compliment a win, whenever possible**. In a team setting, coaching goes so much better when spending a little time complimenting the team on what went well. Complement the process, even the goal, if warranted. Everyone will be so much more engaged if they can feel good about some aspect of their work. The posture is then set -- the team feels "the coach is with me."
	14. **Amplify energy.** Find the energy and help tie it to next steps. Take a look, see if the team is agreeing. are they focusing on the right actions? Ask for their takeaways and the 2-3 things they are going to do. Does it match what the coaching has expressed?

Be visionary AND practical	15. **Paint a picture of an enormous vision**. Steve Jobs often described his vision to "put a dent in the universe." Well that's big, bold and aggressive. Mankind may never be able to actually dent the universe, but Job's intent was clear. His statement is just too big and aggressive to have tangible meaning … which is the whole point. Setting a HUGE vision, beyond moonshots, will inspire people to do greater work than they ever imagined possible. Get your teams to set that large unachievable vision. And then stand back and watch what happens. Hint … it will be good. 16. **Make courage contagious.** Great coaches model courage and make it a transitive property. Great coaches describe, model and request courage. "Go big" requires courage. 17. **Point at the ideal and push for the best results**. A coach that berates the individual and tells them to do better can, depending on the circumstance, be worse than useless. But a coach that points to the ideal possible future and inspires specific steps toward that ideal can be a life-changer.

Be giving	18. **It's not about being right.** Be careful. The focus is what the team needs, not what the coach may need. The coach needs to be a guide to a shared realization, not an opinion factory. Keep your own opinions and biases out of the discussion. Then people will be more open to receiving coaching on any future issues they run into.
	19. **Teach 'em, a lot of them**. Early on Bill Campbell realized he couldn't work 100 hour weeks. He had to figure out a self-scaling algorithm. How many people can you reach as a coach? If you help others learn to coach, will that create the fan-out you need? Develop a plan. Bill Campbell did, teaching the teacher, developing others as coaches.
	20. **Use inquiry** - We all know inquiry is useful, but is it a practical tool for influencing? Yes! Inquiry and storytelling are the two primary communication mechanisms to engage mentees. It is time to accept this reality: lecturing or long-winded advocating are a waste of time. Sticking with inquiry and anecdotes make for palatable and sticky learnings.
	21. **Check the issue**. Remember to do a check: Is the stated issue the right thing to help with? Is it actually the big issue? Sometimes the real issue or struggle is a layer or two down, so use inquiry to dig it out.
	22. **Allocate time to think.** For example, "Let's each of us take 5 minutes and write down 5 ideas each on the whiteboard" can be effective. Often a team needs to go broad, so this activity can be a key. Then talk through the ideas. If it is time to narrow, you can ask, "OK, what are the key criteria? OK, let's run the ideas through the criteria." Then you can work it through and "do it together" with the team.

23. **Go around the room**. If it's a team you have there, then coach the team. Ask to go around the table and hear from each member of the team. The talkative folks often dominate the more quiet folks. This may not lead to the best result.

24. **Personalize**. When coaching the team, you may find different issues are affecting different people. Work to uncover whether there is a debate. The team's anointed speaker, often a Product Manager or team leader, may have different ideas than the rest of the team.

25. **"Do it together."** Instead of telling people the answer, or telling them what to do, talk it over in the meeting and have them work it through themselves, with guidance. An example I saw was Scott Cook coaching a team trying to gain clarity on their product's value. He asked them, "you have someone in the elevator and you can only say 2 or 3 things to have them want your offering, what are those thing you would say?" He then led the team through creating the statement of three key things. They did it together. As a result, the team saw how to craft a thoughtful, focused, statement of customer value.

26. **Help folks find their passion.** Steve Jobs said, "I read something that one of my heroes, Edwin Land of Polaroid, said about the importance of people who could stand at the intersection of humanities and sciences, and I decided that's what I wanted to do." We know Steve found his passion. As a coach, you have a unique opportunity to guide people to their own realizations.

Resource: Legal Checklists for Fast Experimentation

From: Christine Chen
To: Patty Porter
Subject: The Prizmic Labs Experimentation Fast Path

Our Prizmic design principles for fast experimentation are here to make it simple to test straightforward solutions in non-regulated spaces!

Riskier experiments (using PPI, credit card charges, etc.), can be a little slower to deploy, but are more secure for good reason … and we'll help you run those experiments too.

Two key things to understand are out dat stewardship principle snad our Fast-track-experimentation checklists.

Prizmic Data Stewardship Principles

Our Prizmic data stewardship and governance principles reflect our corporate values especially the "integrity come first, we all win-together then follows". We realize that the principles must be simple to follow. Therefore at Prizmic our principles for data stewardship are -

- Help customers improve their personal and business lives with customer data. So we help them manage their lives, live and work efficiently, save money, be more productive, and live within all regulations.
- Choiceful approach. We give customers choices about Prizmic use of data that identifies them.
- Openness and clarity. Prizmic gives open and clear explanations about use of data.
- Publish or share only aggregated, unidentifiable data. And only in ways that identify no individuals.
- Train Prizmic employees about data safety and security. We also educate our customers about how to keep their data secure.

Fast Track Rapid experimentation: no approval needed checklists!

Below the 3 types of fast tests employees can run: Dry Test, Prototype, and Pilot. If your test conforms to checklist for each test type, you can run the test with no legal team approval required:

1. Dry test

   - Test run with fewer than 30k external testers for less than 2 months

   - No other product offers as part of test (helps keep revenue recognition clean)

   - Apply all Prizmic data stewardship principles to protect customer data

   - Ask for first 4 numbers of the user's credit card but don't collect all numbers

   - Stay in compliance with US consumer tax regulations

   - Comply with Prizmic branding and naming experimentation principles [see Resource:Protecting our brand]

   - Limited to users in US, CA, IN, SG, AU, NZ, BR

2. Prototype

   - Test run with fewer than 30k external testers for less than 2 months

   - Prototype does not actually complete financial transactions or collect cc data

   - No other product offers as part of test (helps keep revenue recognition clean)

   - Collects only non sensitive data needed to run test

   - Not targeting governmental agencies or employees in test

   - Apply all Prizmic data stewardship principles to protect customer data

   - Ask for first 4 numbers of the user's credit card but don't collect all numbers

- Testers may be given small token for their time
- Stay in compliance with US consumer tax regulations
- Comply with Prizmic branding and naming experimentation principles
- Limited to users in US, CA, IN, SG, AU, NZ, BR

3.   Pilot

- Fewer than 1000 testers for less than 3 months
- No fee charged
- Not in or near regulated areas like money movement, healthcare, childcare, or consumer tax outside the US,
- Collects only data needed to run test
- Not targeting governmental agencies or employees in test
- Apply all Prizmic data stewardship principles to protect customer data
- Ask for first 4 numbers of credit card but don't collect all numbers
- Testers may be given small token for their time
- In compliance with US consumer tax regulations
- Comply with Prizmic branding and naming experimentation principles
- Limited to users in US, CA, IN, SG, AU, NZ, BR

If you do not meet these no-approval-needed experimentation guidelines, contact us at prizmiclabs@prizmic.net, we're here to help!

Resource: Protecting Our Brand With "Prizmic Labs"

Hi there all you grassroots innovators who are creating new experiments (which, with the right pivots and insights, will become our home run innovations of the future).

Prizmic Labs®

The Word of the Day is: Prizmic Labs.

We're talking brand baby! Using the Prizmic Labs brand solves a multitude of problems that we, as a premier innovation company that is continuously pushing out new early-phase customer experiments, really do need to solve.

Here is the list of issues the Prizmic Labs brand solves:

1. How to make it clear something is not representative of all Prizmic mainstream products?
2. How to free our innovators to create inexpensive and light experiments without feeling they have underachieved and moved too quickly?
3. How can a customer have the right expectation for breadth and depth of functionality?

Prizmic Labs differentiates full-fledge Prizmic branded offerings (think PrizmView, Prizm Appointments, P-Lightbeams, Prizmation, etc.) from early experiments (think Done-a-Day, Prizm On Fleek, etc.). Please use the Prizmic Labs brand on anything that fits in this category.

How to:

For the more detailed look at using the brand and site (Prizmiclabs.com) for experimentation, here are some guidelines:

Prizmic Labs - the new incubation brand for early innovations

BENEFITS of using the Prizmic Labs brand – Lightweight Process

1. PROTECTION. Using the Prizmic Labs brand on Whitespace time Experiments that are still proving love metrics protects our corporate brand, boosts customer trust, and helps all our stakeholders.

2. MINIMIZED Legal Guardrails. To help teams move fast as they run their dry tests, pilots or prototypes, or even dry tests with concierge back-ends, you don't have to speak to legal.

3. Easy NAMING Process. When you use the Prizmic Labs you can bypass some legal requirements, such as trademark and naming, so you can get started faster. Just use a short descriptive name of what it does or the benefit, ie. 'Bill Pay' or 'Tax Preparer' with no adjectives – and you don't need to get a trademark search or involve legal in the naming. And in order to optimize transition to mobile world, keep to 12 characters or less.

4. RAPID HOSTING Environments / Minimized Security Guardrails. When you use Prizmic Labs as your brand and get an approved Prizmic Hosting Environment, you can also get an x.Prizmiclabs. com vanity URL, and bypass CIS. This is fast and easy (typically within 24 hours), especially when using Prizmic Labs.

5. SANDBOX TESTING. For experiments that innovate around our core offerings or use sensitive data, sandboxes might meet your hosting needs.

TESTING and Reaching Users

Today there are many options for testing with customers, from formal to scrappy in-person testing (malls, airports, etc.), unbounce.com with registration page, Craigslist ads, Webex, and other techniques. If you need help in getting to customers, go to the "Design thinking" section of the Prizmic labs microportal to learn more.

When you get customers to test with, particularly useful types of Minimum Viable Products are -

1. A PRE-MVP. First of all, not even an MVP, the pre-MVP is learning by doing Interviews, ethnography, observation, and contextual inquiry. These activities gather surprises that may be synthesized into patterns, themes and then insights.

2. The FAKE-O-BACKEND. With the Fake-o-backend, the app appears to be real, a nice high quality user experience, and the hypothesized area of key customer values seems to work! But the human equivalent of hamsters on wheels are running around in the background, making the service or "magic" happen.

3. DRY TEST. A wonderful, clear, high polish description of the service appears on a page, and user's sign up, taking measurable digital action to show intent. But absolutely nothing real exists beyond the landing and sign-up pages.

4. CONCIERGE. In this MVP a person walks the customer though the experience delivering the key value for the customer. Nothing real is built, but the customer receives the hypothesized value, and the concierge has figured out how to put together and deliver the value.

Resource: The Prizmic Enterprise Grand Challenge

From: Walter Hicks

To: All_Hicks_Staff_Global
Subject: Our Grand Challenge at Enterprise Division

Folks,

We've decided to help better focus our next Hack Days and Whitespace competition series by establishing a Grand Challenge as our "thematic foundation." Grand Challenges can help us in three key ways:

- To focus on what's most important,

- To envision bold leaps forward, and

- To drive results that exceed expectations.

Here's how I think about Grand challenges: They declare a bold vision, and state an ideal metric (measurable, but so aggressive it may never be achieved). A Grand Challenge also states the benefits delivered to the customer.

Truly great Grand Challenges tend to inspire greatness because they push the cognitive process beyond what feels "normal". The targeted benefit, whether to customers, society, humanity or the world in general, may be so powerful that it demands contemplation. The ideal metric may seem so outlandish that the sanity of the issuer is questioned. The gulf between current reality and the Grand Challenge's target may be so large as to intimidate.

Based on your input and discussion with my staff, our Enterprise division Grand Challenge for this fiscal year will be the following:

- **Vision**: Customers are up and running with Prizmic Enterprise in

one day, zero effort
- **Ideal Metric:** Our customers expend zero resources and effort, and we enable "100% enterprise ready" status within a day (remember this is the 'ideal')
- **Intermediate Metric:** Reduce customer deployment time to 50% of current (achievable, our immediate target)
- **Grand Challenge:** Innovate new ways to move us closer and closer to the Ideal.
-

Effective immediately, we will reserve the lionshare of special recognition and rewards for the projects that most directly focus on our Grand Challenge using Whitespace Time .

P.S. For further reading and inspiration, here are some example Grand Challenges (that my staff and I love!) -
- Google search
  - Vision: You get one answer
  - Idea Metric: The perfect answer comes, instantly
  - Customer Benefit: You have **the** answer
- The Bill & Melinda Gates Foundation's 'Eradicate Malaria" Challenge
  - Vision: The world is free of Malaria
  - Ideal Metric: 0 cases of malaria
  - Benefit: Health!
- Khan academy challenge
  - Vision: Provide free education to the entire world
  - Ideal Metric: Every human has access to the education they desire
  - Benefit: Educated world, better life for all
- John F Kennedy's Moon shot challenge
  - Vision: Send a person to the moon and return them to earth safely
  - Ideal Metric: Moon landing, earth landing, no injuries
  - Benefit: Inspire humanity

CPSIA information can be obtained
at www.ICGtesting.com
Printed in the USA
BVHW052304121118
532691BV00021B/132/P